Unequal Conflict

Unequal Conflict

The Palestinians and Israel

John Gee

OLIVE
BRANCH
PRESS

An imprint of Interlink Publishing Group, Inc.
New York

First American edition published in 1998 by

OLIVE BRANCH PRESS
An imprint of Interlink Publishing Group, Inc.
99 Seventh Avenue • Brooklyn, New York 11215 and
46 Crosby Street • Northampton, Massachusetts 01060

Published simultaneously in Great Britain by Pluto Press

Library of Congress Cataloging-in-Publication Data
Gee, John, 1953–
    Unequal conflict : the Palestinians and Israel / John Gee.
      p.   cm.
    Includes bibliographical references and index.
    ISBN 1–56656–303–8
    1. Arab–Israeli conflict. 2. Israel–History. I. Title.
DS119.7.G3878 1998
956. 04–dc21
                                   98-3189
                                      CIP

Printed and bound in Finland

Contents

To Dorothy

Introduction

Only the more observant and knowledgeable traveller notices the monuments which line the road from Israel's Tel Aviv international airport up to Jerusalem. After passing between extensive fields, it begins to ascend into the higher lands which lie to the east. At this point, over to the north, a tank sits atop a four-sided column. This is the monument honouring the Israeli soldiers who fell in a vain attempt to wrest the Latrun salient – astride the Tel Aviv–Jerusalem road – from Arab forces in 1948. Wooded hills close in as the journey proceeds. Some way on, rusted vehicles lie at the roadside. Dates painted on them show that they are not the detritus of traffic accidents, but vehicles wrecked in Arab ambushes in 1948. Further on, a sign points the way to a nearby hill. It is the site of Qastel, an Arab strongpoint whose capture by the Haganah (forerunner of the Israeli army) after a week-long battle in April 1948 was a decisive moment in its battle for control of the Jerusalem road. Soon afterwards, the road enters the city which Israel has proclaimed its capital. These are the more visible monuments, commemorating the sacrifices and victories of the Jews of Palestine during what they remember as Israel's War of Independence.

The Palestinian Arabs, who were the major losers in that war, have their own memories of 1948. For them, that was the year of al-Naqba – 'The Catastrophe'. The road to Jerusalem, a city they too claim as their capital, is also lined with monuments for them, although most are rather less visible than the Israeli ones. The Palestinians call the airport not 'Tel Aviv', 'Ben Gurion' or 'Lod', but Lydda, the Arab name by which it was commonly known before the creation of Israel. In the hills just east of the Latrun monument stood the villages of Yalu, Beit Nuba and 'Imwas. The Israeli army captured them at the beginning of the June 1967 war. Israel recalled the bitter struggle for the Latrun salient in 1948, and resolved to ensure that the area would never be restored to Arab sovereignty. As a first step, it expelled the 10,000 villagers, destroyed their homes and seized their lands. Now the trees and picnic areas of Canada Park cover the site of 'Imwas, but the Palestinians know what once stood there.[1]

Palestinians remember that Qastel was home to a human community, now gone, as well as a battle site. This was where Abd al-Qadir al-Husseini, the foremost Palestinian military leader in 1948, was killed. Further on, as the road approaches the outskirts of Jerusalem, the still substantial remains of the village of Lifta are visible on the slopes of the valley to the north, while nearby, there is a turning to the south to Giv'at Sha'ul. Lifta was another Palestinian village whose inhabitants were expelled 50 years ago; most now live north and east of Jerusalem, some on land that belongs to Lifta but which remained beyond Israel's grasp until 1967: now they have Jewish settlements as neighbours.

Giv'at Sha'ul used to be the Jewish neighbour of Arab Deir Yassin. It was here that the most notorious atrocity carried out by Zionist military forces in 1948 occurred. On 9 April, members of the Irgun Zvai Leumi and LEHI (widely known as the Stern Gang) killed at least 170 people, mainly after the village fell to their attack. Most traces of Deir Yassin have been obliterated and an extension of Giv'at Sha'ul (Giv'at Sha'ul Bet) stands on its site. The absence of any commemorative marker to the villagers who died has not erased the recollection of what happened at Deir Yassin from Palestinian memories.[2]

Such opposing perspectives extend to the entire land of Palestine/Israel and to all of its history. At a time when Israelis can celebrate 50 years of their state's existence and the realisation of a large part of the Zionist dream, Palestinians think of what they have lost and a nightmare of dispossession come true. These feelings were not mitigated by the signing of the Declaration of Principles (DoP) by Israel's Prime Minister, Yitzhak Rabin, and Palestine Liberation Organisation (PLO) Chairman, Yasser Arafat, in September 1993, or by subsequent agreements.[3] Arafat has repeatedly assured Palestinians that his intention is to secure the creation of an independent Palestinian state, with Jerusalem as its capital, but the prospects for that happening seem remote.

The Palestinians have passed through a similarly grim period before, in the decade and a half after the Catastrophe of 1948. There was despair then, but there were also people who tried to learn from the past and to work out how the Palestinian people might take charge of their own destiny. If this is a time of gloom and demoralisation, it may also become a period when Palestinians seek once more to draw lessons from their history, in the hope that they will illuminate a way to a happier future.

The present work considers that past. It presents the interpretations of an outsider, but one who has worked in solidarity with the

Palestinians for over 30 years. I believe that has given me some insights upon which I can now draw. It is not my intention simply to recount the history of Palestine, but to offer a critical perspective on the Palestine/Israel conflict which I hope might advance debate on how the Palestinians came to be in their present situation.

My central aim is to consider the reasons for the successes which Zionism and the State of Israel have had in their struggle with the Palestinian people. Past attempts to do this by Palestinians and those sympathetic to them have tended to highlight great power support for Zionism as the reason for its victories. While the crucial part this has played is not to be denied, it must also be recognised that Zionism and the society which it created in Palestine have always had considerable strengths of their own which they brought to bear in the conflict with the Palestinians. It is also necessary to face up to the weaknesses in the Palestinians' society and leadership which contributed to undermining their efforts to resist a determined and ruthless enemy.

The protracted Palestine/Israel conflict was an unequal one from the beginning. Those who played the major role in building the State of Israel came from countries transformed by industrialisation, scientific progress, expanding education systems, political revolution and reform: they were 'modern' in senses in which their Palestinian adversaries were not. Palestinian society was changing before its first encounter with Zionist settlers, but was still overwhelmingly pre-industrial. Old social norms and relationships remained strong. The traditional order in Palestine left its Arab population ill-equipped to face the onslaught of a determined movement of colonisation from the modern capitalist world. They have been in a position not unlike that of other peoples in the Americas, Africa, Asia and Australasia who in earlier times found themselves overwhelmed (with few exceptions – notably Japan, which adapted successfully) by European colonisers. Once the Palestinians acknowledge this unpalatable fact, it will be easier to begin to pinpoint ways of redressing the imbalance of power between the two sides, so that a time may come when the Palestinian Arabs are able to live in their homeland alongside Israeli Jews, not as second class citizens of a Jewish state, or as residents of a subordinate entity, but as a free and equal people.

1

Independence and Catastrophe

The formation of a negative image of an enemy is a natural consequence of any conflict. It occurs spontaneously as a result of the injuries which each side inflicts upon the other, but the image is often shaped and manipulated by the leaders of the opposing sides in order to mobilise their people for combat. It is easier to fight an enemy who is perceived as an inhuman aggressor and a threat to one's own rights and existence than a foe who is seen to have similar basic aspirations and ideals to oneself. Human beings can more readily inflict harm upon others when they have come to regard them as inferiors rather than people acknowledged to be equal in dignity and rights.

Engaging in a conflict imposes another requirement on the adversaries which runs counter to the creation of propaganda images. This is the need to know one's enemy in order to counter that enemy's strengths effectively and take advantage of any weaknesses.

The Palestine/Israel conflict has produced much negative propaganda material on both sides. There have also been serious studies undertaken by Israeli and Palestinian scholars on the conflict and various aspects of it. The fact that they have points of view which reflect their national and political affiliations does not detract from the value of the best of their work.

From Palestinian perspectives, a number of writers, the best known being Edward Said, have written clear and well argued works on the Palestine/Israel conflict.[1] There are also many well researched books and papers on aspects of the conflict such as the expulsion of the Palestinians in 1948, the conduct of the Israeli authorities towards the Palestinians under their rule whether since 1948 or since 1967, Palestinian politics and Palestinian national identity.[2] There remains a crucial gap, however. Palestinian scholarship on the internal dynamics of Israeli Jewish society and Israeli views is largely notable by its absence.[3] Such work as has been undertaken has often suffered from the effort to accommodate it to an ideological framework (Israeli work on Palestinian society, by contrast, is plentiful, but suffers from the same defect). The problem is even worse outside a small circle of relatively open minded intellectuals.

At the popular level, there is no interest in understanding Israeli society or its thinking; if, as an outsider, one suggests that there might be good reasons for taking such an interest, one frequently finds oneself confronted with a response which equates understanding with approval. Many Palestinians instead give credence to tales which reflect badly on Israeli society, whether they have a basis in fact or not.

For years, it was commonly held among Palestinians that, in the meeting chamber of the Knesset (Israel's parliament), there was a large map on the wall which showed an Israel which extended from the Nile to the Euphrates – the borders, it was believed, to which Israel aspired. Similarly, the two narrow blue bands above and below the Shield of David on the Israeli flag were said to represent the two rivers to which Israel one day intended to expand its frontiers. In the mid-1980s, I recall being told that air hostesses on El Al airplanes had adopted a uniform based on traditional Palestinian garments and that it was described as 'Israeli national costume'.

None of these stories had any foundation. Photographs of the inside of the Knesset building have been publicly available since it was opened and visitors – including pro-Palestinian individuals from non-belligerent countries – could visit the Knesset, so that the facts could have been ascertained easily: the notorious map did not exist. Basic information distributed by the State of Israel offered a perfectly cogent explanation for the blue bands on the flag: they were inspired by those edging the traditional Jewish prayer shawl. As to air hostesses in Palestinian dresses, a trip to any airport in the world from which El Al operated could have confirmed that that story was untrue. (It died quickly, unlike the other two.)

Tales like these not only reflect popular Palestinian suspicion of Israel, but something rather deeper: a sense that Zionism and the State of Israel have two agendas. One, Israel declares to the world: the other is rather more sinister. This is not without foundation – states frequently present themselves as acting on a high-minded and moral basis while pursuing sordid and immoral policies in reality. However, this interpretation of Zionism and Israel has been taken to extreme lengths. The rise of Zionism and the creation of Israel are seen in conspiratorial terms, as if removed from the normal dynamics of history. Conspiracies there have been – it would not be unreasonable to identify Israeli collusion with Britain and France during the Suez crisis in 1956 as one example – but this general approach has provided an easy substitute for a real effort to understand the imperatives driving those Jews who embraced Zionism during its early history or the dynamic factors propelling the development of the society created by Zionism in Palestine.

What is more alarming than the existence of such attitudes at the mass level is that they extend to much of the Palestinian leadership. In spite of the availability of a superabundance of publications on Israel and the existence of a body of knowledgeable Palestinian intellectuals upon whom they could call for help and advice, Palestinian political leaders sometimes reveal astounding misconceptions about Israeli society and politics.

An obvious example is the status long accorded by the PLO to Neturei Karta. This is an organised body of 20,000 strictly observant Orthodox Jews whose main communities live in Jerusalem, the Tel Aviv suburb of B'nei Brak, New York and London. Strongly anti-Zionist, they consider Zionism and its creation, the State of Israel, to be abominations. In their view (once common to all the strictly Orthodox), the ingathering of the Jews to the ancient Jewish homeland is to be consequent upon the coming of the Messiah, sent by God to the Jewish people, who have meanwhile forfeited the land because of their non-adherence to God's commandments. Zionism blasphemously went against God's design and usurped the Messiah's role. Neturei Karta therefore rejected participation in any Zionist body, including all the institutions of the State of Israel, and they refuse to carry Israeli passports. They condemn everything which they regard as the evil consequences of Zionism, including the treatment suffered by the Palestinian Arabs.

In July 1994, Yasser Arafat, as President of the PNA, appointed Rabbi Moshe Hirsch as his Minister for Jewish Affairs. Rabbi Hirsch is responsible for Neturei Karta's external relations. It is understandable that the Palestinians should value the stand taken by Neturei Karta and that they have, on occasion, pointed to their position as evidence that not all Jews support Zionism. What is more questionable is the political weight which some PLO leaders have given to what is, after all, a small minority among religious Jews.[4]

While such behaviour may reflect appreciation of the position taken by Neturei Karta over the years, it also suggests a lack of understanding of Israeli society. Some 80 per cent of Israeli Jews are not in the least bit religious: on the contrary, most of them are deeply resentful of the influence of the religious minority upon their political system and way of life. When Yasser Arafat looks at Neturei Karta, he sees Jews who support the Palestinians: when the majority of Israelis look at ultra-Orthodox Jews of any description, they see representatives of an alien and backward way of life of which they want no part. Besides revealing a misunderstanding of Israeli society, this stand towards Neturei Karta may also be a reflection of the low level of priority which Palestinian leaders attach to seeking to cultivate support among the Israeli public, or at least, to soften their hostility.

Statements by Palestinian political organisations setting forth their views on the nature of Israeli Jewish society are yet more revealing of a failure to understand that society and the people who make it up other than as dispossessors and oppressors of the Palestinians. In the early days of the re-emergent Palestinian national movement, during the 1960s, the declared political positions of these organisations stressed the artificial character not only of the State of Israel, but also of any concept of Jewish nationhood, whether in Israel or elsewhere. They also dwelt on the alleged conspiratorial character of Zionism and its alliance with and subservience to imperialism:

> ‹Claims of historical or religious ties of Jews with Palestine are incompatible with the facts of history and the true concept of what constitutes statehood. Judaism, being a religion, is not an independent nationality. Nor do Jews constitute a single nation with an identity of its own; they are citizens of the states to which they belong.

So stated Article 20 of the Palestine National Charter, as amended by the Palestine National Council (PNC) in 1968 and maintained as the PLO's basic statement of aims – in spite of the de facto supercession of many of its clauses by subsequent policy changes – until 1996.[5]

According to Fatah, the major Palestinian organisation within the PLO since 1969, the intention of Theodor Herzl, at the 1897 *Basle Congress*:

> was the creation of a Zionist movement which would endeavour to establish a fanatic Jewish state by usurping the land of Palestine from its people and granting it to the alien people without a land.
>
> This plot was masterminded by Herzl; Chaim Weizmann, his successor as head of the Zionist movement; and Britain, the

state that pretended to be our ally in our struggle for independence. Their aim was to gain control of Palestine and thrust its
people, about to reap the fruits of their struggle for freedom and
independence, back into the gloom of occupation.[6]

The Popular Front for the Liberation of Palestine (PFLP) stated:
'That Israel constitutes a colonialist expansionist presence at the
expense of Arab land and its owners is not a matter for discussion.
For us it is the tangible experience before which all spurious claims
and allegations fade away.'[7]

> [A] basic strategic line in our war with Israel must aim at
> unveiling this misrepresentation [of the Palestinian struggle as a
> racial war against the Jews – my note], addressing the exploited
> and misled Jewish masses and revealing the conflict between
> these masses' interest in living peacefully and the interests of
> the Zionist movement and the forces controlling the State of
> Israel.[8]

Subsequently, especially after 1974, when the PLO made its first
move towards defining its goal as a state alongside Israel in the
West Bank and Gaza Strip, PLO organisations had less to say about
the character of Israel than before, but the views articulated earlier
have lived on up to the present day, even among those who regard
Israel as an established reality in the Middle East.

The problem is not that all these views are wrong, but that they
represent an oversimplification of reality and betray a failure or
refusal to comprehend the motivations which drove the early
Zionists and the dynamics of Israeli society today. There are
Palestinians who have acquired a better understanding of these
things, partly through close contact with Israel and its institutions
– and often against their wishes. They include Palestinian citizens
of Israel (many of whom speak Hebrew well) and a handful of
intellectuals, scattered around the world, but their expertise has
been little utilised by the national movement.

The Islamist organisations which have come to prominence
since 1987 have an even less insightful approach to Israel. The
Charter of the Islamic Resistance Movement (Hamas) treats the
Palestine conflict as one in which the adversary is the Jews as such.
It embraces the worst anti-semitic conspiracy theories, claiming
that Jews control the international media through their wealth
and are behind a succession of revolutions, the First World War,
the Freemasons and Rotary and Lions Clubs. They are also said to

be behind the Second World War and the foundation of the United Nations 'in order to rule the world through that organisation'. The Charter goes on to say that:

> the Zionist plan has no bounds and after Palestine they wish to expand from the Nile River to the Euphrates. When they totally occupy it they will look towards another, and such is their plan in the *Protocols of the Learned Elders of Zion*.[9]

Such characterisations of an enemy inevitably had practical consequences. Palestinian leaders have tended to overstress the role of external support for Israel and have underestimated the internal strengths of the society which Zionism created in Palestine. In denying the claims of that community to nationhood and stressing its colonial character, Palestinian leaders from the 1920s onwards underestimated the attachment which the people who made it up had formed to their new homeland. Many believed that, once under serious pressure, the Jewish settlers' determination would wilt and they would re-emigrate en masse.

While Palestinian nationalist organisations have, since the mid-1960s, referred to divisions within Israeli society – notably between Jews from the Arab countries and those of European origin – their skin deep analysis has not been followed up strategically or tactically in any serious way. For example, Palestinian armed actions have generally drawn little distinction between different groups of Israelis in order to complement a political strategy of cultivating support (or at least, mitigating opposition) among certain sections of the population. Bombs and armed attacks in the 1960s and 1970s simply targeted Israelis who could be reached, with no sign that an attempt was being made to distinguish between rich and poor, Oriental or European and little effort to discriminate between civilians and the military. Hamas's approach, at its crudest, does not even distinguish between different elements at a theoretical level: it can only reinforce Israeli-Jewish national solidarity against the Palestinians.

Zionism and Jewish Society in Palestine

The Enlightenment and the French Revolution at the end of the eighteenth century set in train far-reaching changes in Europe. They gave a great impetus to the emancipation of the Jews, who acquired most or all of the rights of other citizens, apart from in

Russia. New opportunities opened up in the worlds of academia, business and politics, which many Jews seized with enthusiasm. For most, emancipation not only meant the end or the mitigation of old forms of oppression by non-Jews, but also freedom from the authority of Jewish religious leaders. They could escape from what seemed like a strait-jacket of enforced religious observance and circumscribed knowledge and slip into a new world of possibilities. They took with them as much or as little Judaism as they wished. A small proportion became Christians, but most did not embrace any other religious faith. Secular Jewish intellectuals may have rejected much of traditional Jewish religious belief, but they often carried with them a legacy: the exacting analysis and attention to detail of Marx, Freud and others were surely influenced by a religious Jewish tradition which attached great importance to such qualities.

Jewish emancipation and secularisation threw up a conceptual problem which had not existed before: that of Jewish identity. Hitherto, it had been very clear what a Jew was: a Jew was an adherent of Judaism. Such a definition became more and more problematic with the decline in Jewish religiousness. By the mid-nineteenth century, the strictly Orthodox were a minority among European Jews. In what sense were people whose ancestors had practised Judaism but who were themselves agnostics or atheists Jewish? Was there any way in which a Jew who converted to another religion remained Jewish? Orthodox Judaism could answer these questions according to its own criteria,[10] but they would not satisfy either non-Jews or non-religious Jews.

Ideas of nation and race which developed in the nineteenth century provided alternative definitions. A new strain of anti-semitism arose in Europe, borrowing, but significantly different from, the older Christian variety. It was often strongest among the more chauvinistic European state-builders, wary of national differences and keen to homogenise their societies to conform with the values of the dominant nationality within the nation-state. For this ideological current, Jews belonged to a race with inherent characteristics and as such, remained Jewish even if they ceased to practise Judaism.

Nineteenth and early twentieth century secular Jews were not necessarily averse to the concept of a Jewish race.[11] The idea that human beings were divided into distinct races was largely taken for granted in all developed societies and the notion that those races had characteristics which gave them a higher or lower status within a racial hierarchy was certainly widely accepted. It was one of the ideological underpinnings of European imperialism. Where

Jews, for the most part, dissented from anti-semitic non-Jews was not on general principles, but on the ascription of inherent negative characteristics to Jewish people which conferred upon them an inferior racial status to non-Jewish Europeans. Most would not question the assumption that 'races' of a darker hue were inferiors.

A secular Jew looking back at the previous hundred years from the vantage point of 1880 would have had considerable cause for optimism about the future. Almost all the changes affecting Jews during that time were in the direction of greater liberty and a better quality of life. It seemed that there was no reason to assume that things would not continue to improve. The outlook changed for the worse in the next two decades. The assassination of Tsar Alexander II of Russia in 1881 was followed by pogroms in which hundreds of Jews were killed or injured by anti-semitic mobs. They recurred on a smaller but no less violent scale during the decade and a half leading up to the First World War – most notoriously at Kishinev in 1903, but also following the 1905 Revolution. Anti-semitism was used by the Tsarist regime quite deliberately to meet the challenge of liberal reformers and revolutionaries alike: such was its influence among the more benighted parts of the Russian people that to brand opponents as Jews or their agents conspiring against Mother Russia was an effective weapon. It was the Tsarist secret police who concocted *The Protocols of the Learned Elders of Zion*, supposedly the outline of a Jewish conspiracy to achieve world domination.

Anti-semitism in Russia might have been written off as one expression of that country's general backwardness compared to the rest of Europe, but developments elsewhere were not reassuring. In 1895, Karl Lueger was elected mayor of Vienna. His Christian Social Party combined anti-semitism with an enlightened programme of social reform: both proved popular. In France, the Dreyfus case exposed a strong streak of anti-semitism in what was regarded elsewhere in Europe as one of the most enlightened and tolerant societies in the world. Such manifestations of anti-Jewish hatred undoubtedly shook the hopes of many who had once thought anti-semitism would soon be a thing of the past. One of those who felt this way was Theodor Herzl.

As a journalist working for the Viennese newspaper, *Neue Freie Presse*, Herzl was keenly aware of events in the Austro-Hungarian Empire's capital city, but it was the Dreyfus case which had the biggest impact upon his views, making him, as he would say later, a Zionist. It was precisely because strongly anti-semitic views were expressed by a sizeable segment of what he believed to be an enlightened society that Herzl was so shocked. He was now convinced of the deep and essentially unalterable nature of the hostility of the rest of humanity towards the Jews amongst them. What they therefore needed, he concluded, was a state of their own, overwhelmingly Jewish in population and with a Jewish government. He articulated this view in his pamphlet, *The Jewish State*, and argued for it in letters, articles and speeches.

Zionist groups and ideas had already existed for half a century, but Herzl systematised previous proposals and added ideas of his own to create a workable scheme. Herzl's personal qualities were suited to the task he now undertook: that of establishing a permanent Zionist organisation and furthering its goals. He had clarity of purpose, determination, energy, organising ability and diplomatic skills which would be needed not only in pursuing the backing of non-Jews, but also in bringing together Jews already sympathetic to Zionism, whose views frequently differed sharply. Within a few years of writing *The Jewish State*, he succeeded in bringing together a diffuse collection of individuals and groups into a truly international Zionist political movement. Its objectives were summed up briefly in the statement of aims which the First Zionist Congress adopted at Basle in 1897.[12]

At that first congress, around 200 people gathered in the concert hall of the Basle Municipal Casino. They heard Herzl declare, 'We want to lay the foundation stone for the house which will become the refuge of the Jewish nation.' At the end of the three-day meeting, the delegates adopted the document which would become known as the Basle Programme:

Zionism aims at the creation of a home for the Jewish people in Palestine to be secured by public law.

To that end, the Congress envisages the following:

1. The purposeful advancement of the settlement of Palestine with Jewish farmers, artisans and tradesmen.
2. The organizing and unifying of all Jewry by means of appropriate local and general arrangements subject to the laws of each country.
3. The strengthening of Jewish national feeling and consciousness.
4. Preparatory moves towards obtaining such governmental consent as will be necessary to the achievement of the aims of Zionism.

For 50 years, the Basle Programme defined the objectives and broad strategy of the Zionist movement. It pursued them doggedly. The Palestinian Arabs, by contrast, have never succeeded in defining a shared set of aims and a strategy for realising them and then working to implement them over decades; indeed, as will become apparent, their movement has frequently been characterised by its want of political clarity and a failure to agree and persist for long with any strategic course.

A few significant points about the Basle Programme and the discussions around it may not be immediately obvious today. In the first place, it was not entirely candid about the central goal of Zionism. Defined as a 'home for the Jewish people in Palestine', the real aim was to achieve nothing less than a state. There was no confusion in the minds of those assembled at Basle on this point. For a small and weak movement to declare outright that it sought a Jewish state in Palestine would be politically unwise. Palestine was part of the Ottoman Empire, whose rulers could not be expected to be tolerant of Jewish settlement in that land if they believed that it would ultimately lead to Palestine being detached from the imperial domains. Nor would any European power at that moment in time endorse what would be seen as the open advocacy of the amputation of part of the Ottoman Empire by the Zionist movement. This was an early demonstration of the preparedness of the Zionist mainstream to project as its goal an objective which others would deem reasonable, in order to deflect opposition, without for a moment relinquishing its real strategic aim. (In more recent times, the Israeli right has claimed to foreigners that Israel needs to hold large areas of the West Bank and Gaza Strip for 'security reasons', when in fact, it was ideologically committed to the retention of land it maintains to be Israel's by right, irrespective of any security consideration.)

The Basle Programme provided for the pursuit of the Zionist goal on diplomatic and practical levels. The search for backing for a Jewish state would go on simultaneously with the construction of a new society in Palestine. Thus, even while Zionist leaders discussed Palestine's future with other political leaders, the basis for negotiating its fate would be subtly transformed by the gradual accumulation of Zionist strength on the soil of Palestine. This remains very much a feature of Zionist practice: since the 1993 Israel–PLO agreement, Israeli governments have engaged in talks about the future of the West Bank and Gaza Strip at the same time as attempting to determine their outcome in advance by expanding settlement in the areas they wished to retain.

A third point worth noting is that while the Basle Programme only refers to the 'settlement of Palestine' by Jews, Zionists at this time readily described this process as 'colonisation'. The term had not yet acquired negative connotations. In the Europe of the 1890s, the colonisation of other lands was considered to be not only justified, but also a praiseworthy and noble enterprise, taking civilisation to backward lands, conferring benefits upon their existing inhabitants (if need be, against their will) and developing the unexploited resources found there for the greater good of humanity. Colonisation seemed to offer a chance for the industrious poor and the persecuted of Europe to better their lot and they went in their millions to the USA, Canada, Australia, New Zealand, South Africa and other lands during these years. In this respect, Zionism was born as a child of its time. Its great misfortune historically was that it appeared on the political scene at the apogee of colonialism, rather than earlier, and therefore had to cope with a world becoming steadily more critical of the colonisation of the global South by Europeans.

Fourthly, the absence of any mention of the Arab inhabitants of Palestine in the Basle Programme was highly significant. At that time, they made up well over 90 per cent of the country's population. The writer Israel Zangwill coined the slogan, 'The land without a people for the people without a land', but it is impossible to accept that anyone who had so much as bothered to glance at a contemporary travel guide could be under the illusion that the land was empty. Consistent with their European colonialist outlook, the early Zionists did not consider the existence of another people in Palestine to be significant except in so far as it proved to be an impediment to the realisation of their hopes. The land was 'without a people' only in the sense that those who lived there were not accorded the dignity of being a people, with opinions and rights worthy of consideration on an equal basis. This outlook would remain fundamental to Zionism. It might have emerged in the 1890s by default – a natural outgrowth of the attitudes of the time – but it would remain psychologically and politically necessary to the fulfilment of Zionist aims in the years to come.

The founders of modern Zionism believed their goals to be laudable, humane and just. They certainly did not set out to harm anyone. Yet it would be impossible to achieve those aims without injuring those who stood in the way of their realisation. In its single-minded pursuit of the Jewish state, the Zionist movement was never prepared to allow the Palestinian Arabs to veto the fulfilment of its objectives, which would have been the only way to avoid a clash with them.

If the Palestinian Arab presence could be denied, then it followed that no one could be seriously wronged by the creation of the Jewish state; if it had to be admitted that other people did exist in Palestine, then their claims to constitute any form of coherent society, especially one which asserted its right to national self-determination, had to be belittled and denied. To accept them would have meant bringing into question the legitimacy of the Zionist programme: Zionism might exist as a theory, but as a practical project it would be stillborn.

The readiness of the dominant trends in Zionism to pursue their objectives irrespective of Palestinian Arab wishes was undoubtedly a strength, whatever its ethical ramifications. The desire to have both the moral high ground and a Jewish state in a land whose people rejected it has resulted in the creation of a vast array of justificatory arguments unparalleled in subtlety and imagination by the ideological products of any other colonising movement, as will be demonstrated below.

The Basle Programme called for the 'obtaining such governmental consent as will be necessary to the achievement of the aims of Zionism', and subsequently, considerable energy was invested in efforts to win great power support. Crude leftist and Arab nationalist analyses have suggested that this indicates that Zionism put itself at the service of imperialism, or to take a different tack, that it sought to manipulate great powers to achieve domination of the Arab world. The hard fact was that, in the face of the opposition which might be anticipated from the Palestinian Arabs, great power support would be needed if Zionism was to prevail. What was always sought, however, was a marriage of convenience; the central goal of achieving and building up a Jewish state was what counted and it was to be an independent state, not anyone's puppet. A hundred years on, that state is a reality. In spite of its heavy reliance on US support, it has a keen sense of its own distinct interests.

Zionism had a programme after Basle and it quickly developed an organisational structure. During the next few years, institutions which would play a vital role in the implementation of the Basle Programme were founded – most notably, the Jewish National Fund (JNF), established in 1901 to acquire land for exclusive Jewish use and settlement. Wherever Zionist organisations existed, they sought to broaden their support within Jewish communities, as well as to win the sympathy of non-Jewish opinion formers and political leaders. Thus, Zionism not only embraced contemporary European notions concerning nationhood, the state and colonisation: it also organised itself in the fashion of Europe, with well defined political structures and chains of responsibility and accountability. Zionist political organisations had branch-based structures, debated policy and held elections. Zionist congresses heard reports, reviewed work, adopted resolutions and elected officials. Sectoral organisations for women and youth were established. There were many possibilities of work for activists, whether skilled or unskilled, with plenty of time to spare or very little: everyone could feel that he or she had a part to play. Zionism developed as a movement capable of embracing adherents of a wide variety of political views and social backgrounds, with affiliated bodies in practically every country where there was a Jewish community of European origin.

The international character of the Zionist movement was a result of the dispersal of the Jews which Zionism sought to reverse, but it was a positive factor when it came to seeking support. Every country of Europe or settled by Europeans had Jewish populations who spoke its national tongue as their own first language, or at least, a good second language. The Zionists among these communities were also generally familiar with the workings of their country's political system, as well as institutions such as the trade unions and press. They could rally support using a shared language to express their case in terms which their local audience could readily understand. These were assets which the Palestinian Arabs simply did not possess. While there have certainly been many instances of Zionist bodies or individuals seeking to exercise influence on decision making and public opinion in an underhand way, the great majority of Zionist activity has been legal and at least as open as that of any other political trend in democratic countries.

In the demonology of most Islamists, as well as of some Arab nationalists, Zionism appears to be a monolithic power, representing the world's Jews. This has never been true. Even at the highest points of Jewish identification with the State of Israel, such as at its creation or during the 1967 war, there have been Jews, religious and secular, who have dissented publicly or privately from the dominant trend. In spite of this, one of Zionism's achievements has been to present itself as representing the aspirations of all Jews even when it did not.

Zionism was, in fact, a minority political trend among Jews until the Second World War. In Western Europe and the USA, most secular Jews saw their future in terms of advancement within their home countries. In Eastern Europe, where anti-semitism was most acute prior to the rise of Nazism, Zionism was at its strongest and it was this region (above all, the areas which had been part of the Russian Empire before the First World War) which would furnish the Zionist movement in Palestine with the bulk of its leadership and the State of Israel with its political and social elite. Nevertheless, Zionists were outnumbered by adherents of socialist organisations, including predominantly non-Jewish parties and the Jewish Bund and also by religious Jews, deeply hostile to socialism and Zionism. Among Jews in the Arab world, Zionist ideas were virtually unknown before the First World War and found little sympathy thereafter. Even the rise of Nazism did not create a Jewish majority for Zionism. It was the Nazi attempt to exterminate Europe's Jews which did that. It convinced most Jews that the Zionist case for a Jewish state was right, but it also disproportionately devastated the ranks of the opponents of Zionism: whereas scores of thousands of European Zionists had acted upon their beliefs and gone to Palestine, the socialist and religious millions who remained in Europe – along with those Zionists who had stayed – were largely exterminated by the Nazis.

Far from being a movement representing all Jews, pre-Second World War Zionism had to wage a hard struggle against religious and secular anti-Zionist Jews for the hearts and minds of Jewish communities. Its triumph over Arab resistance was preceded by its victory over Jewish opposition under the impact of Nazi genocide. World-wide (apart from in the Arab countries), Zionists became leaders of Jewish community organisations and leaders of Jewish community bodies became Zionists. To Western politicians such as Balfour and Churchill, Zionist leaders had presented themselves as speaking for 'the Jews': it was only in the 1940s that they could do so with justification. But dissent has never gone away. It has been met by intense hostility, no doubt because anything seen to undermine the equating of Zionism and the Jews was regarded as extremely harmful to the former's pretensions. Jewish critics of Israel and Zionism have been branded as 'self-haters' and some have even faced physical intimidation, but the dissident element lives on and grows, even if most dissent now takes the form of alienation from Zionist activity, rather than active opposition.

Palestinian Arabs and Palestine

Writers of Zionist sympathies have portrayed Palestine prior to modern Jewish colonisation as a backward land. They paint a picture of a country which, since the dispersal of the Jews by the Romans, had been transformed from the 'land flowing with milk and honey' to a sparsely inhabited wasteland of desert and marsh. The society which existed there was seen as one stagnating in its own conservatism, corruption and ignorance. In their version of history, it was Jewish settlement which brought progressive change, reclaiming neglected lands, introducing modern European farming methods and invigorating the local economy with an infusion of capital. This is not the place to examine such claims in depth, but some rebuttal is necessary.

Since ancient times, previously wooded areas of the Middle East have undoubtedly suffered deforestation and the diversity of the region's flora and fauna has decreased under the impact of human activity. This was not due, as anti-Arab and anti-Muslim writers would have it, to the culture and outlook of the seventh-century Arab conquerers and their successors. The region has undergone at least 5000 years of environmental degradation as a consequence of human activities which resulted, for example, in the collapse of the economies of the city states of Sumer, in lower Mesopotamia, whose irrigation of the land eventually led to the concentration of salt in the topsoil and the end of their agricultural productivity long before the Arabs appeared on the scene. Warfare (especially that of the period of the Crusades) and the marginalisation of the Ottoman Empire in the world economy following the rise to global pre-eminence of Western Europe in the sixteenth and seventeenth centuries also played their part in the process of destruction: it is simply ahistorical and unjust (to put it mildly) to ascribe the backwardness of the Middle East's economy at the turn of the twentieth century to the influence of Islam and the supposed defects of the Arab temperament.

Testimonies to the backwardness and squalor of Ottoman Palestine by European visitors which were subsequently used for their own ends by promoters of the Zionist cause must be put into perspective. Visitors' accounts varied a great deal, even when describing the same place. Questions need to be asked about what the more condemnatory eyewitnesses expected or wanted to see: a nineteenth-century Western Christian's opinion of what the land described as 'flowing with milk and honey' ought to look like might well have borne as much resemblance to the ancient reality as the same person's image of Jesus and the disciples (blue-eyed and fair-skinned) did to how they would actually have appeared.

Palestine under Muslim rule enjoyed varied fortunes. From the end of the sixteenth century, it suffered, like other Ottoman territories, from the declining fortunes of the state as a whole. The decay of central authority, the consequent increase in lawlessness, including bedouin raids on settled communities, and the exactions of tax farmers combined to bring about a decline in the area of land under cultivation, abandonment of villages in insecure locations and a fall in the absolute size of Palestine's population. This process reached its nadir at the end of the eighteenth century, but thereafter, a revival began.

Sultan Selim III, though overthrown in 1807, had initiated a series of efforts by the Ottoman government to modernise and reinvigorate the Empire. These culminated in the period of the Tanzimat (Reorganisation) from 1839 to 1876. All aspects of the Ottoman state were affected by the reforms and they had significant consequences for Palestine. They reinforced the authority of the Ottoman central government, which, with its reorganised and strengthened army, was able to enforce its authority in Palestine over powerful local leaders and the bedouin. Tax farming was abolished and an effort was made to encourage cultivators to bring more land under cultivation.

From 1856, when the Crimean War ended, there was growing contact with Europe as more visitors came and the European churches expanded their activities. The economy began to grow steadily. Palestine's main exports to Europe before 1882, when the first Zionist settlement was established upon its soil, were wheat, barley and dura, sesame, olive oil, soap and oranges. Between 1856 and 1882, the volume of wheat exports through the port of Jaffa increased five times; the number of oranges exported grew from six million in 1857 to 26,250,000.[13] The overall trend of exports was strongly upward. One indicator of the increased prosperity of Palestine at this time was the growth of its population, which rose from about 350,000 in 1850 to about 470,000 30 years later, despite losses caused by conflicts with the authorities in the 1860s, a severe cholera epidemic in 1865–66 and the disruption brought about by the levying of men for military service in the 1876–78 Balkan war.[14]

In short, Palestine was developing and growing in prosperity before the advent of Zionism: it was not a wilderness awaiting the fructifying benefits of Jewish colonisation. This is not simply a matter of historical interest. One of the justifications offered by

Europeans for their colonisation of other regions of the world was that they made far better use of these lands than did their backward indigenous peoples; Zionism took shape when such ideas were current and it assimilated them. Tales of reclaiming marshland and 'making the desert bloom' would be used as tools to legitimise the wrenching of the land from its indigenous population. The undoubted improvements in the health and incomes of most Palestinian Arabs after the beginning of Zionist colonisation would be cited to prove its benefits, thus further legitimising it in the eyes of its supporters and others. In reality, improvements were afoot before the advent of Zionism and those which followed were generally not consequent upon any positive contribution by it.

Palestinian Society

At the end of the nineteenth century, Palestine was still an overwhelmingly agrarian country. About two-thirds of its people lived in villages, but the urban population also relied heavily on the rural areas for its livelihood. A significant part of its income was ultimately generated by rents and taxes gathered in the country areas; shopkeepers and craftsmen supplied goods needed by peasants, but urban dwellers also purchased produce brought to market by peasants. In some towns, such as Hebron, many urban dwellers owned and farmed land nearby.

Palestinian rural society was close-knit and insular. People were deeply attached to the area in which they lived and knew it intimately: minor geographical features which in modern-day Israel have become anonymous often had names when the Arabs were there. Women embroidered dresses with patterns peculiar to their own region – a tradition maintained today by refugee women long exiled from the land that nurtured and moulded them.

The *hamula* (often translated as clan) was a crucial social reference point. This was a grouping of families believed to be linked by a common male ancestor. A small village might be inhabited by members of just one *hamula*. It could help to provide its members with security – economic or physical. Wealthier members might be expected to lend a helping hand to those less fortunate and to be generous on festive occasions, such as at weddings. In the face of an external threat, the *hamula* would seek to defend its own. The most prominent members assumed representative functions in dealings with the authorities or other clans. The *hamula* reinforced itself through marriage within its ranks, which helped to keep property and land rights within the group. This frequently involved matches between cousins; considerations of romantic love or the perils of repeated reproduction from within a limited genetic pool did not figure.[15]

In this society, notions of individual standing and responsibility existed, but not in a modern Western sense: clan identity and responsibility counted for a lot. If a person murdered a member of another *hamula*, that would often lead to a violent feud between the clans of the two individuals concerned, which would last until some form of settlement was agreed. Any male member of the offender's clan ran the risk of being killed by the victim's clan and violence could escalate alarmingly.

This notion of collective responsibility extended to the regulation of public morality and, above all, to that of women's behaviour. If a woman became the subject of talk suggesting she had engaged in immoral sexual activity, it was expected that a male relation, such as her father or brother, would kill her, as her behaviour was held to reflect upon the family's honour. Society in general saw the killing as justified and treated the murderer with respect. Such practices have become less common, but they still exist. It has proved easy to cast aspersions on a woman's conduct and this has been used to weaken women's participation in the national struggle and in efforts to win their rights within Palestinian society.[16]

Class differentiation existed alongside and within the clan structure, but was influenced by it. It was the prominent families of traditionally powerful clans who were the major landowners and who formed the urban elite, such as the Husseinis, Nashashibis and Khalidis in Jerusalem, the Abd al-Hadis, Tuqans and Jarrars in Nablus or the Shawwas in Gaza. From these families were drawn local officials, including governors, under the Ottomans and they continued to furnish leaders under successive administrations right up to the present day, as a glance at a list of West Bank mayors under Jordanian and Israeli rule reveals.

As suggested by some of the foregoing observations, Palestinian society was very male-dominated. A woman from a poor family married in her teens and lived a life of unremitting toil and repeated pregnancies. She had no access to education or power and was very much subject to the wishes of her husband and his family, although her standing rose with the arrival of male children and advancing age.

Religion exercised a deep influence on the lives of all communities in Palestine – and still does – governing the rituals surrounding birth, marriage and death, providing an annual calendar of events to be marked, including Ramadan and 'Id for Muslims and Christmas and Easter for Christians, which were marked at different times according to denomination. Muslim figures such as the Mufti of Jerusalem and Christian bishops and priests were treated with great respect and could act as leaders because of the status they enjoyed. Religion penetrated people's day to day lives, a small sign of this being the way God is still readily invoked in conversation – 'Al-Hamdulillah' (Thanks be to God) and 'Inshallah' (God willing) being phrases which spring to Muslims' lips. In the third quarter of the nineteenth century, about 83 per cent of Palestine's population was Muslim, between 11 and 15 per cent were Christian and the remainder were Jews or Druzes.

Palestinians were generally tolerant towards each other in matters of religion. Had Western powers found an occasion to intervene in Palestine under the pretext of protecting indigenous Christians (as France did in Lebanon in 1860), they might have been expected to seize upon it, but no such chance occurred: Muslim–Christian tensions arose from time to time, but never became serious. The threat of Zionism later acted as a stimulus to Muslim–Christian solidarity. One of the first responses of the Palestinians to the changed situation created by British rule after the First World War was to form Muslim–Christian committees in the major cities to represent the common views of Palestinian Arabs to the new rulers.

This society was facing new pressures and strains in the second half of the nineteenth century. The majority of those who made their living from the land were poor. They practised subsistence farming. The Tanzimat reforms eased their tax burden, but many were encumbered by debt, which was manageable in years of good harvests, but not in bad years. The Ottoman authorities, and later the British, made some small efforts to ease this problem, but most debt remained owing to userers who charged extortionate rates of interest – often around 30 per cent a year.[17] When peasants could not keep up payments, they faced eviction and the loss of their livelihood. Population growth only exacerbated this problem, producing increased pressures on limited land. It was quite common for a poor family to be unable to survive by working its own land and for members to work as hired labourers elsewhere. This now happens on a larger scale as a result of the Israeli seizure of Palestinian farmland within both Israel and the areas occupied in 1967: many villages inside Israel especially have been 'proletarianised' as people deprived of land have been forced to become labourers for Israeli Jewish enterprises.

The greatest beneficiaries of the expansion of agricultural production and exports in the nineteenth century were the larger landowners in areas near the coast, where the bulk of the market-stimulated increase in productivity occurred, mainly through bringing new areas into cultivation rather than through innovations in technique and technology. It was normally only the larger owners who could afford to commit resources to the expansion of cultivation and take the risks involved in switching crops. Palestine's increasing prosperity and the expansion of its education system, including the teaching of more non-religious subjects, stimulated the country's intellectual life.[18] The political leaders, writers and journalists who emerged from the existing urban elite groups were to play an important role in expressing and shaping the views of the Palestinian Arabs as their confrontation with Zionism unfolded.

This was the society which would face the challenge of Zionism. Its qualities and faults can be discussed in their own right, but the crucial question that has to be asked is: To what extent did the nature of their society help or hinder the Palestinian Arab people's resistance to Zionism?

The Conflict Unfolds

The first modern Jewish agricultural settlements were established by existing Jewish communities in Palestine at Petah Tikva and Rosh Pinna in 1878. The Jewish presence on the land expanded with the arrival of the immigrants of the First Aliya (1882–1903)[19] following the pogroms in Russia in 1881. Most new settlements were set up on land bought by the Jewish Colonization Association (later known as the Palestine Jewish Colonization Association – PICA) founded by Baron Rothschild. PICA's purchases were chiefly made from absentee landowners and this remained true even under the British Mandate until 1930.[20]

A few colonies were, like Rosh Pinna, established deep inland, but the major concentration was in the coastal plain, where it had been possible to buy land in large parcels. This was where settlements such as Zikhron Ya'akov, Hadera and Nes Ziyyonah – now major Israeli towns – were founded. Much of the coastal region was marshy and malarial, and had been insecure until recently, which explains why it was thinly populated by Palestinian Arabs compared to the hill regions inland. It would take a considerable commitment of resources to reclaim it for farmland. The poor majority of Arabs could not afford to invest either the money or the time required, but the new Jewish settlers, subsidised by Rothschild and other benefactors, set about the task with enthusiasm. They paid a heavy price as disease took its toll. Life was hard: even the Baron's largesse only stretched to allowing the settlers the means to subsist. They soon discovered that they could achieve more at a lower cost by making use of the labour of people more inured to the hardships of the area – the local Arabs.

A pattern emerged in the relationship between these settlements and local Arabs. At first, they encountered hostility from the tenant farmers who were evicted from the land purchased by Jewish organisations, as well as from neighbours wary of the newcomers' intentions. Then, as they hired Arabs on a regular basis for reclamation and farm work (including individuals displaced to make way for them) and began to buy goods from their neighbours, they gradually gained acceptance. A few friendships were formed and some Jews even learnt Arabic and took to wearing Arab clothes.[21]

This was to change following the creation of the Zionist Organisation. The immigrants of the Second Aliya (1904–14) came mainly from Russia, following the failure of the 1905 Revolution, when the authorities fell back on the tried and tested tool of anti-semitism to counter the left. Most of those who went to Palestine combined firmly held Zionist beliefs with socialist ideals. The majority re-emigrated, but among those who stayed were individuals who were to play leading roles in the struggle to establish and build a Jewish state, including David Ben Gurion, Levi Eshkol, Berl Katznelson, Yosef Weitz and Pinhas Sapir. The new arrivals were very critical of the older settlements – above all, because of their use of Arab labour. They believed that this diminished their capacity to absorb Jewish immigration and also preserved a pattern of social relations which they regarded as a negative feature of diaspora Jewish life.

Arthur Ruppin, who left Germany to settle in Palestine in 1908, was to be the architect of Zionist settlement policies during the British Mandate. He had visited many of the existing Jewish settlements on a trip in 1907, and as head of the Palestine Office established by the Zionist Organisation, he acquired a profound appreciation of their achievements and limitations. Ruppin pointed to a fundamental problem faced by would-be Jewish settlers. He acknowledged that the Palestinian Arab peasants (*fellahin*, in Arabic) had a standard of living superior to that of their counterparts in neighbouring countries, but noted:

Yet there still remains a considerable difference between the essential conditions of life of the Palestinian fellah and those of the migrating European Jews. The Jew is ready to suffer many hardships, but he cannot, if he is to remain healthy, descend below a certain minimum, both in quality and quantity of food. He cannot do without schools and medical attention for his children, and he will not degrade his wife to a beast of burden. His consumption of soap, laundry, clothes, light, etc., is far greater than that of the fellah, which is practically nil. To put it shortly: *Even in Palestine the Jew wishes to remain a product of the twentieth century.* He will not let himself be pushed back to that level of culture which Europe has left a hundred years behind, and which has only survived in the East. This is perfectly intelligible, yet it presents an extremely difficult problem. It must be remembered that the Jews only form a small minority in the country, and that they cannot in one day induce the non-Jewish majority to adopt a higher standard of life. It is true that the standard of the Arab is also slowly rising, and that in the course of a few decades the difference between them and the Jews might perhaps disappear. But in this period of transition the Jew in Palestine stands confronted with this competition, wherever he may settle. It is characteristic that after all only those Jews who, like their non-Jewish competitors, have employed cheap native labour, have hitherto drawn any profits either from industry or agriculture. This fact that the Jews *wish to maintain in Palestine a European standard of civilisation and must yet compete economically with a majority not accustomed to such a standard*, contains the root of all the difficulties with which our agricultural colonisation has to struggle, and which has not been fully mastered up to the present day.[22] (emphasis in original)

Ruppin summed up what he had learnt from the experience of the First Aliya colonies:

In the year 1908, when the Zionist Organisation made their first groping steps into the region of colonisation, the object was clear: it was to provide with the least possible expenditure a permanent agricultural existence for the greatest number of Jews, an existence which would enable them to lead the life of civilised men and would also seem desirable to their children. How was this to be attained? Only one thing was clear: both forms of colonisation known in Palestine in the 25 years before 1908, namely plantations on the one hand, and extensive wheat cultivation on the other, did not lead to its achievement. Plantations are unsuccessful because they require too much capital, and because they use far more non-Jewish than Jewish labour, extensive wheat cultivation because the Jewish mentality cannot conform to its monotony, and the small produce is not enough for a European minimum of existence.[23]

Ruppin was no socialist himself, but his analysis of the faults of the older colonies and his opinions about future models of settlement dovetailed neatly with those of the Zionist left. Like Ruppin, they saw the diaspora Jewish social structure as an inverted pyramid, top heavy with merchants and businessmen, beneath which were strata of professionals such as doctors and lawyers, intellectuals, artisans and, finally, a tiny group of workers and farmers. The left shared with many non-socialist Zionists the goal of establishing a society in Palestine in which the Jews would be a 'people like other peoples', which meant, among other things, reversing the pyramid: building a society with a broad working-class base.

The socialists of HaPoel HaTzair, founded in 1905 (one of the chief components of what is today the Israeli Labour Party), believed that the marriage of Zionism and socialism could produce a society in which the interests of Jewish workers would be paramount. Hashomer Hatzair (later the predominant component of Mapam, the Marxist-Zionist party, founded in 1948) differed in believing that the Jewish working class would have to *take* power in the future Jewish state and sought to place themselves in a position to lead that struggle as the state's foundations were being constructed. The Zionist leftists called for 'the conquest of the land' and 'the conquest of labour' – for Jewish workers to take on all work on Jewish-owned land and all work in Jewish-owned enterprises, which meant that Palestinian Arab workers would be excluded from employment in the Jewish sectors of the economy.

Prior to the establishment of the British Mandate and mass Jewish immigration, it was difficult to realise these aims. The established Jewish settlements were resistant to them, but a beginning was made. It would be simplest to insist upon exclusively Jewish labour in new settlements founded by people who believed in it as a matter of principle. In 1909, the first kibbutz was founded at Degania, to the south of the Sea of Galilee, soon to be followed by Merhavyeh, Kinneret and others. These were collective settlements, in which land was held in common and all shared the tasks of production and the fruits of their labour. From the outset, they were exclusively Jewish in membership, and have remained so up to the present day. The kibbutz assumed an important role in the Zionist project, even though kibbutzim have only ever been home to a small proportion of the Jews of Palestine/Israel (about 3 per cent today). They could absorb more immigrants than farms based on individual ownership and extensive farming. Moreover, they were soon recognised as having a particular value as the struggle for control of the land of Palestine intensified:

Of all the types of settlement, the kibbutz is, in its structure, closest to a military formation. The problem of family maintenance is solved within a general organizational framework and through a common effort; the age composition of the kibbutz, and especially in a young kibbutz – a high percentage of young people and a low percentage of the aged and children – increases its power and military strength. It has an advantage over the military framework since the kibbutz member does not spend his life in the same atmosphere of boredom which makes even the best of armies deteriorate in peacetime or in times in which there is no intensive training. Also, this form of living does not cut a person off from his family life, as does the army. It is true that the kibbutz does not possess the external military discipline ... but this disadvantage is compensated for by the inner discipline of kibbutz members and their consciousness of the national value of the role entrusted to them.[24]

It is not surprising that kibbutz members have furnished a significantly greater proportion of the Israeli army's officers and soldiers in elite units than their percentage within Israel's population, and have taken the combat casualties that went with it.

After the British government's Peel Commission made the first proposals to partition Palestine into Jewish and Arab states in 1937, the Jewish Agency saw the desirability of expanding Jewish settlement into new regions with a view to demanding their inclusion within any future Jewish state resulting from partition. When, consequently, there was a drive to found settlements in the north Negev and Western Galilee, it was kibbutzim which were established – in the circumstances of the time, in close liaison with the Haganah, the principal Zionist military force. In all, 149 kibbutzim had been founded by the time the State of Israel was established.

Kibbutz members were generally well educated and highly motivated. The kibbutzim formed themselves into federations aligned with political parties, which saw them as a base for the spreading of their own influence. Kibbutzim belonging to Hashomer Hatzair formed HaKibbutz HaArtzi in 1927. HaKibbutz HaMeuchad, founded the same year, was aligned with a section of what later became the Israeli Labour Party. In time, a handful of religious kibbutzim were established.

The collectivism of the kibbutzim was not to the taste of all who wished to live on the land. Another form of settlement was developed by and for them in the 1920s, also based on the exclusion of non-Jewish labour. The moshav was a co-operative settlement. Land was distributed between its members on an equal basis and each family farmed its own allotted portion. The moshav as a unit arranged credit and organised wholesale purchase of goods and marketing of moshav produce. Most moshavim were aligned with the dominant labour Zionist trend in the Yishuv, but, as the moshav, unlike the kibbutz, was not anathema to the Zionist right, a few moshavim aligned with anti-socialist tendencies developed. The first moshav was Nahalal (birthplace of Moshe Dayan), founded in 1921 by a group who had left Kibbutz Degania. In all, 77 moshavim were established between 1921 and 1948: many more were set up afterwards, when their population outstripped that of the kibbutzim by far.

Most Jewish immigrants settled in towns, either those which grew up from the older Jewish settlements or in Jerusalem, Haifa and Tel Aviv, founded to the north of Jaffa in 1909 and destined to become the largest Jewish population centre in Palestine. Large scale immigration began only after the First World War. Conditions were harsh and Jewish settlement faced Arab opposition. The Palestinian Arabs mainly made their feelings known by peaceful means, whether through representations to the Ottoman government or articles in the Arabic press, notably *al-Karmil* and *Falastin*, but there were also violent incidents. Most Jews seeking refuge from lands of persecution chose to go to the USA: between 1881 and 1924, when Congress closed the door to mass immigration, 2.5 million Jews migrated there from Eastern Europe,[25] compared to a net Jewish immigration of under 90,000 to Palestine during the same period.

Zionism's fortunes changed following the First World War. The Ottoman Empire participated in that conflict as an ally of Germany. In 1915, Britain made commitments which, in the understanding of the Arab side, meant that, following the war, it would support the creation of an independent Arab state, of which Palestine would form part.[26] In 1916, by the secret Sykes–Picot agreement, Britain and France agreed to share the bulk of the

Ottoman Empire between themselves and their allies after victory. On 2 November 1917, British Foreign Secretary A.J. Balfour sent a letter to Lord Rothschild which contained the declaration which has since been known by his name:

> His Majesty's Government view with favour the establishment in Palestine of a national home for the Jewish people, and will use their best endeavours to facilitate the achievement of this object, it being clearly understood that nothing shall be done which may prejudice the civil and religious rights of existing non-Jewish communities in Palestine, or the rights and political status enjoyed by Jews in any other country.

The caveat concerning the rights of 'the existing non-Jewish communities in Palestine' gave a deceptive appearance of fairness to the Balfour Declaration. Whereas 'the Jewish people' were to have a 'national home', the Arab 90 per cent or so of Palestine's population were defined negatively, as 'non-Jewish communities', and any term which implied that they had a claim to nationhood or national rights was deliberately avoided.

The Balfour Declaration had the appearance of a statement issued unilaterally by the British government, but in fact, it was the result of five months of drafting and negotiation involving Zionist leaders (headed by Chaim Weizmann), Balfour and the British Cabinet.[27] The Zionist quest 'to obtain such governmental consent as will be necessary to the achievement of the aims of Zionism', as the Basle Programme stated, had attained its first great success. This was a triumph for Zionist diplomacy and in particular for Weizmann. He had laboured for years to build up contacts in the British establishment. An important early convert to Zionism was C.P. Scott, editor of the *Manchester Guardian*, whose support opened many doors. Weizmann's achievement highlights the advantages which the Zionist movement had over the Palestinian Arabs in dealings with Western states. He had lived in Britain since 1904 and was familiar with British politics, values and views. He spoke to British politicians in terms which they could readily grasp (for example, mentioning to Lloyd George that Palestine was a small mountainous country not unlike Wales), but he also understood that it was important to persuade them that it would be to Britain's advantage to support Zionist aims.

Britain gained military control of the whole of Palestine as Ottoman power collapsed in 1918. When, in 1922, the League of Nations awarded the Mandate for Palestine to Britain, its provisions incorporated the Balfour Declaration. Thus it also acquired the validation of that world body.

Britain ruled Palestine from 1918 until 14 May 1948. Throughout this time, it faced Zionist and Palestinian efforts to influence its policy. Zionist pressure aimed at securing the fulfilment of the 'National Home' pledge contained in the Balfour Declaration, which meant seeking to open Palestine up as much as possible to Jewish immigration, opposing any legal constraints upon Jewish land purchasing, calling for British protection against violent Arab opposition and opposing any constitutional concession to the Palestinian Arabs which might strengthen their ability to impede the fulfilment of the goals of Zionism. The Palestinian Arabs opposed the implementation of the Balfour Declaration from the first. They were against anything which would strengthen the Zionist position, particularly Jewish immigration and land acquisition.

Britain sought to give the impression of following an even-handed policy of seeking to protect the rights of both Jews and Arabs in Palestine. On occasion, Arab pressure did win concessions from Britain, but overall, British policy favoured Zionism. British rule enabled the Zionist movement to create the preconditions for establishing a Jewish state. At its foundation, Zionism was a movement based outside Palestine. Jews (including non-Zionists) made up under 10 per cent of Palestine's population. Had Britain, following the First World War, accepted that the principle of the right of nations to self-determination applied to the Arabs of Palestine and proceeded to prepare the country for independence at an early date, there can be no doubt that the Zionist enterprise would have been halted in its tracks by Palestinian Arab opposition. But Britain, quite deliberately, did not follow such a policy.

In a letter to the Prime Minister, Balfour explained:

The weak point of our position, of course, is that in the case of Palestine, we deliberately and rightly decline to accept the principle of self-determination. If the present inhabitants were consulted they would unquestionably give an anti-Jewish verdict. Our justification for our policy is that we regard Palestine as being absolutely exceptional, that we consider the question of the Jews outside Palestine as one of world importance.[28]

Britain insisted upon 'balancing' the claims of the Palestinian Arabs not against the small Zionist Jewish minority in Palestine, but against the supposed claims of Jews world-wide, as represented by the Zionists. In consequence, it persisted with the 'Jewish

National Home' policy up to 1939, with only occasional waverings. Even after issuing the 1939 White Paper, which went some way towards meeting Palestinian Arab demands, its enforcement of its provisions was not determined: for example, land purchases by the JNF continued in areas where they were officially banned and these were legalised after the State of Israel was proclaimed.[29]

Under British rule, in spite of a high Arab birthrate, the proportion of Jews in Palestine's population rose to nearly a third through immigration. Jewish land ownership grew from 2.04 per cent to 7 per cent, but, concentrated in particular regions and strategic areas, it provided a territorial basis for establishing a state. The economic, institutional and military foundations of Israel were created during the Mandate, mainly with the active support of Britain. By the time Britain made its inglorious exit, the balance of power in Palestine had tipped decisively in favour of Zionism.

Institutional Foundations

Shortly after the beginning of British rule in Palestine following the First World War, the Jewish Agency was created according to the terms of the Mandate for Palestine approved by the League of Nations. These terms had been drafted in consultation with the Zionist Organisation. Article 4 stated that:

> An appropriate Jewish agency shall be recognised as a public body for the purpose of advising and co-operating with the Administration of Palestine in such economic, social and other matters as may affect the establishment of the Jewish national home and the interests of the Jewish population in Palestine, and subject always to the control of the Administration, to assist and take part in the development of the country.

The Zionist Organisation was recognised as the 'appropriate Jewish agency'. An attempt was made to enhance its claim to representative status in 1930 by expanding the Agency to include non-Zionist Jews, but nothing really changed. Over time, the Jewish Agency for Palestine took on the character of a Zionist government in waiting. Other national institutions already existed or were created: political parties, the Histadrut (Jewish labour federation), organisations of agricultural settlements and the Vaad Leumi (People's Council), representing the organised Jewish community in Palestine. The Palestinian Arabs, by contrast, did not develop strong national institutions during the first decades of their conflict with Zionism and, arguably, not until the rise of the Palestine Liberation Organisation in the late 1960s.

At the onset of the conflict with Zionism, Palestinian Arabs readily identified themselves according to religion; they had a sense of being citizens of the Ottoman Empire and a feeling of affinity with the peoples of the neighbouring lands, with whom they shared a language and culture. They were certainly strongly attached to their clan and the locality where they lived. Elements of a Palestinian Arab national identity co-existed with and some-times incorporated these other self-definitions at the end of the nineteenth century. The indigenous Arabs' sense of belonging to a Palestinian Arab people became steadily stronger, sharpened by the conflict with Zionism, but their national identity was still being formed at the outset of British rule and its character was obscured to the outside world by the tactical demands raised by Palestinians in the first years of British rule for inclusion in a Syrian state and by the fact that the Western world most readily recognised national entities which conformed to Eurocentric defi-nitions of nationhood and national character.[30]

Palestine was given clearly defined borders as a result of the division of the former Arab territories of the Ottoman Empire between Britain and France. Objecting to the imposition of European rule and feeling that they could better resist Zionism as part of a larger Arab entity, the Palestinian Arabs at first expressed a wish to be part of a Syrian Arab state, but the reality of the terri-torial division of the area constrained them to organise and act within the borders of Mandate Palestine. Although attempts were made to co-ordinate responses to the growing Zionist threat and to the imposition of British rule, they failed to create national structures to match the emerging Jewish ones. A series of Palestinian Arab conferences and congresses took place from 1919 onwards, and the third, in 1920, created an Arab Executive under the presidency of Musa Qassem al-Husseini (dismissed as mayor of Jerusalem earlier in the year by the British because of his strongly anti-Zionist stand), but it never established the kind of bureau-cratic machinery and organisational networks which the Jewish Agency had. The Arab Executive collapsed following Musa Qassem's death in 1934: he had been instrumental in holding its disputatious membership together.

Palestinian political parties were formed, but these too could not match the Zionist parties in the extent of their networks or the effectiveness of their structures. The Istiqlal (Independence) party, a pan-Arabist organisation whose Palestinian branch was founded in 1932, managed to build something of a national network of activists, but most parties induced scepticism among Palestinian Arabs. With justification, they were seen as the tools of men who established them primarily to serve their personal interests rather than those of the Arab people of Palestine. The two main political parties in the 1930s were the Palestine Arab Party, established by Jamal Husseini, brother of the Mufti of Jerusalem, Haj Amin al-Husseini, in 1935 and the National Defence Party, which had been launched four months earlier, in December 1934, by Ragheb Nashashibi, the Mufti's chief political rival. The squabbling of the party leaders and the willingness of the anti-Mufti politicians to court British support against their dominant rival did not improve the parties' standing among the people.[31]

An enduring problem in Palestinian Arab society was that the traditionally powerful families saw leadership as belonging as of right to their members. There was no machinery through which a talented person of humble social origins could rise to the top: all depended upon the choices of established leaders and it has often been the case that what counted most for them was not the talent of subordinates, but their personal loyalty.

Assuming prominent roles in large part by virtue of their social status, Palestinian leaders had a markedly different relationship to those they sought to lead than their Zionist counterparts had to their constituencies. Palestinian leaders tended to treat their people – especially the peasantry – as a passive body of followers whose role was to be summoned into action when the leaders chose and demobilised as soon as they had served their purpose. (The fact that the 'followers' sometimes refused to act in this way is beside the point.) The cultivation of popular support was important, but it often took place through patronage, giving favours or posts to influential individuals within a particular locality or *hamula*, rather than through advocating policies and actions around which people would rally. This did not encourage the highest standards of service to the Palestinian Arab people, and it is not surprising that Zionist bodies exploited an elite culture in which co-operation could often be bought to recruit collaborators and acquire land from individuals who, in public, opposed the sale of land to Jews. When the Mufti wished to have his way, he was also capable of using force and intimidation against opponents; other leaders lacked his means.

In contrast, Zionist leaders largely made their way to the top by argument, persuasion and hard work. They needed to demonstrate abilities which equipped them for leading roles. They had to interact with the Jewish public, win support mainly on a political basis and constantly reason and justify themselves. David Ben Gurion, for example, came to Palestine from an East European ghetto before the First World War, and rose to prominence through his work in the Zionist labour movement, to become the leading figure in the Yishuv (the organised Jewish community in Palestine) and first prime minister of Israel. All the way, he had to argue for his views and win support. It was not that there were no Zionist equivalents to the usages of the Palestinian elite, or even to the violence employed by the Mufti: labour Zionists and their right-wing Revisionist rivals used force against each other on numerous occasions in the 1930s and there is little doubt that it was Revisionists (so called because of their demand that the Mandate be revised to 'reunite' Transjordan with Palestine and so make it part of the area of the 'Jewish National Home') who assassinated the prominent labour leader, Chaim Arlosoroff, in 1933. However, these were a much less prominent feature of Zionist Jewish than of Palestinian Arab political life.

The difference in outlook between the leaders of the two communities might be summed up as: Palestinian leaders tended to assume that the people depended upon them (an attitude which they sought to inculcate into their people), whereas Zionist leaders knew that they depended upon their people. The former view encourages estrangement between leaders and people: it fosters dependent attitudes and reluctance to use initiative on the part of the latter. The Zionist models of leadership tended to encourage a dynamic interaction between leaders and led, large scale involvement in political affairs and stronger group solidarity.

Whereas Zionist Jewish society was adept at mobilising all its human resources towards a common goal when necessary, Palestinian Arab society failed to make the best use of its own, not only because of internal rivalries and organisational weakness, but also because of its values. Meritocratic appointment and promotion was the general rule throughout Zionist Jewish society and its public and private institutions, whereas in Palestinian Arab society up to the present time, individuals who would be regarded (not least by those compelled to work under them) as incompetent, unprofessional and indolent have been permitted to occupy responsible posts because they had influential contacts or belonged to a prominent family or faction that someone in a position of authority wished to conciliate.

Giving such people positions in traditional Palestinian society served a function in binding different interest groups together and sharing wealth and power, to a certain extent: such practices helped to make the system work. They were a source of grave weakness once the Palestinian Arabs had to compete with a modern European society which set great store by professionalism, efficiency, time-keeping and achieving quantifiable results. For what had to be achieved by each side in the conflict over Palestine, the administrative systems and values of Zionism were far more suited. It was rather as if a trusty carthorse, well able to pull a heavy load every day, was suddenly challenged to undertake a gallop in competition with a sleek young racehorse: no one would be surprised at the result.

The Palestinian Arabs never managed to match their Zionist opponents in political organisation during the Mandate, with grave consequences for the outcome of the struggle between them. This was not simply a matter of personalities. The main underlying reasons for their different levels of achievement lay in the character of the two societies in conflict. The Yishuv built itself as a democratic (if not particularly tolerant) society and had a loyalty to its nation-building goal which took precedence over all other considerations. Palestinian society had many power structures based on loyalties other than to the national cause and these militated against the development of a genuine democratic life, in which meritocratic advancement would be the norm, and the absolute subordination of all other interests to that of the struggle against Zionism. Had the Palestinian elite gone over to subservience to the British and Zionism, as elites in many colonial countries accepted a subordinate, collaborative role under imperial rulers, it may be that an alternative leadership with a commitment to active popular mobilisation would have displaced them from their dominant role within Palestinian society. But Zionism threatened Palestinian Arabs of all classes, because to realise its aims, it had to take Palestine from its indigenous people, rich and poor, not exercise control over them. While individuals might be bribed or induced to collaborate up to a point, the Palestinian elite as a whole simply did not have the option of abandoning the national cause; they stayed with it and so did the ideological baggage they carried with them.

Under British rule – and mainly with Britain's co-operation – Zionist Jews built not only a shadow government apparatus, but also a largely self-reliant economy, a powerful trade union federation and the nucleus of an army. The Palestinian Arabs were unable to match them. They had no mechanisms for strategic economic planning and private wealth tended to be put into property and trade, rather than industry. The industrial sector of the economy was predominantly Jewish by the Second World War even though over two-thirds of Palestine's population was still Arab. Palestinian attempts to organise labour unions had limited success. The Haifa-based Palestinian Arab Workers Society, led by Sami Taha, was founded in 1922. By 1945, it claimed to represent half the paid Arab labour force, but this was undoubtedly a great exaggeration. It never had democratic elections throughout its existence and scarcely attempted to match the multi-faceted activity of the Histadrut. This largest of the Palestinian union organisations was independent and so faced the hostility of the Mufti, who sought to concentrate power in his own hands. His supporters attempted to set up their own rival union bodies and later, in 1947, it was most likely his men who assassinated Taha. Yet another trade union grouping had been established by dissident communists in 1942.[32]

No Palestinian Arab national military force remotely comparable to the Haganah was built under the Mandate. Fighters were based in their home areas. The Palestinian Arabs lacked the resources and probably the vision to create a trained, flexible, mobile military force which could be directed to where it could be used most effectively, nor did they ever achieve a centralised command structure, able to formulate and direct a coherent military strategy.

While the Zionist movement and Zionist Jewish society in Palestine were male-dominated, women made a big contribution to both. In secular Jewish society, it was normal for women to go out to work, and the institutions of the labour movement prided themselves on their promotion of female participation. Some women took part in Zionist military organisations, although only rarely in combat roles.[33]

Palestinian women contributed much to the national struggle. Women's importance as workers in field and home supporting families tended to be under-rated simply because their labour was unpaid. Women played a key role in educating children in their national culture. However, their degree of active participation in the national struggle was less than it might have been. Palestinian women inside their country have only been mobilised twice on a mass scale – significantly, at the two peaks of the national struggle, during the 1936–39 revolt and in the first couple of years of the Intifada, which broke out in 1987. At those times, the demands made upon men rendered Palestinian society amenable to women taking on new or changed roles, as community organisers, as heads of families in the absence of older menfolk and, during the revolt, as carers for men engaged in armed struggle.

But this was exceptional. Apart from a small minority of educated urban women from the more prosperous families who lobbied the British authorities and organised charitable bodies (some of which played an important social role in the wake of the 1948 catastrophe), women were generally excluded from an active part in the national struggle or kept on its margins by the strong patriarchal value system of their society. A great reservoir of potential strength was severely underutilised. The comparatively greater role allowed to or taken by women in Jewish society undoubtedly helped to compensate for the numerical inferiority of Jews in Palestine as the conflict there intensified up to 1948. In that year, and to a much lesser extent in 1967, women's status in Palestinian society would further undermine its powers of resistance when faced by a Zionist military threat. One reason given by refugees for their flight was that they feared the threat that would be posed to their honour should their womenfolk be left at the mercy of enemy soldiers.[34]

A State in the Making

The Histadrut is usually described as a trade union federation. In fact, it has been much more than that. Today, the Histadrut's full official title translates into English as 'The General Federation of Labour in the Land of Israel'. It was not always thus. It was founded in 1920 as 'The General Federation of Hebrew Labour in the Land of Israel' – an organisation exclusively for Jewish workers. Only in 1966 did it finally drop 'Hebrew' from its title, at the tail end of a protracted process of reform which led to Arab citizens of Israel being admitted to full membership.

From the outset, the Histadrut sought not only to organise Jewish workers on a national basis, but also for national goals.[35] The fulfilment of Zionist hopes in Palestine required more than the simple accumulation of larger numbers of Jewish colonists to change the demographic balance in the country. In the face of Arab opposition, they had to be organised and integrated into state-building institutions. The Histadrut played a vital part in meeting this need.

A mass base for building a Jewish state could only be constituted from Jewish workers, but Ruppin's remarks about the difficulties of employing Jews rather than Arabs on the land applied equally to industrial employment. Kibbutzim and moshavim tackled the problem of how to absorb the maximum number of Jewish immigrants in rural settlements, but, given the limited availability of land, they could only ever take in a small proportion of the new arrivals from overseas. Most would need to be employed in industry and services. However, private employers, like their counterparts everywhere else in the world, naturally preferred cheap rather than expensive labour, which in Palestine, meant employing Arabs rather than Jews.

This was the key problem taken on by the Histadrut. With single-minded determination, it set out to expand the areas of Jewish employment by whatever means were possible. This necessarily meant seeking to displace and exclude Arab labour from employment by Jewish businesses and institutions. This process formed an essential part of the 'conquest of labour'. At first, the Histadrut's position was weak, due to the paucity of Jewish labour in the early years of the Mandate. Appeals were addressed to Jewish employers to take on Jewish workers. Attempts were made to enhance the latter's competitiveness, whether through the provision of Histadrut services (thus reducing the needs Jewish workers had to meet from their earnings) or through securing subsidies from Zionist institutions which would reduce the amount which a Jewish employer would need to find if he hired Jews rather than Arabs. These efforts met with little success.

With the rise of the Nazis to power in Germany, immigration soared, shifting the demographic balance in Palestine and enhancing the Histadrut's power. The two major labour Zionist parties within the organisation had united to form Mapai in 1930, so strengthening its leadership as it (unknowingly) stood on the brink of a period of great opportunities. Its position was further enhanced by the strengthening of its connections with other key Zionist institutions. At the highest level, David Ben Gurion, leader of Mapai, was Secretary-General of the Histadrut until 1935, when he became undisputed head of the Jewish Agency and the most prominent leader in the Zionist movement world-wide.

It was at the onset of the period of mass immigration in the 1930s that the Histadrut launched a more determined drive against the employment of Arab workers in the Jewish sector of Palestine's economy. Jews who employed Arabs faced pickets, intimidation and Histadrut-organised consumer boycotts. Simultaneously, the Histadrut campaigned for Jews to buy Jewish rather than Arab-produced goods (conduct conveniently overlooked by those who later bewailed the Arab states' boycott of

Israel). The effort was successful: the existing vertical division of the economy into Arab and Jewish sectors was deepened and the exclusively Jewish sector expanded. While they were never to be hermetically sealed one from the other, it is not an exaggeration to say that a dual economy existed in Palestine.[36] Hence, the claim that Zionism brought benefits to the Palestinian Arabs through expanded job opportunities can be largely dismissed as self-serving propaganda: the Histadrut strained every muscle to ensure that this did not happen.

The impact of the Histadrut's campaign went beyond the economy. It reinforced territorial divisions, reducing or eliminating the presence of Arab workers and traders in Jewish towns and neighbourhoods. It should not be supposed that this was anything but a policy motivated by political considerations. During the 1930s, the Palestinian economy expanded and rank and file Jewish workers felt less need than previously for a protected niche within it.[37] The initiative for the drive to promote Jewish labour at the expense of Arab workers came from the top and, in spite of occasional declarations of solidarity with Arab labour, any concrete expression of Arab–Jewish working-class unity was quickly stamped upon by the Histadrut. It set up its own department for Arab labour, but that was firmly subordinate to the needs and priorities of the Jewish organisation: it had an appointed Jewish head and its members had no vote in deciding Histadrut policy.

Histadrut activities went far beyond national labour organisation. In the economic sphere, besides incorporating the kibbutzim and moshavim within its structure, it created Hevrat Ha'ovdim (The Workers' Corporation) to set up and operate industrial enterprises and Solel Boneh, a construction company, which built roads and settlements, as well as tendering for contracts in the public sector. Financial backing could be provided by the Histadrut's Bank Hapo'alim (Workers' Bank), whose start-up capital was provided by the World Zionist Organisation.

In the social sphere, the Histadrut organised labour exchanges and a labour school system. It established pension funds and Kupat Holim (The Workers' Sick Fund), which became the chief provider of health care for Jews in Palestine and subsequently fulfilled the functions of a national health service in Israel. (Most Israeli Arabs are members of the Histadrut today because they joined Kupat Holim to gain access to affordable medical care.) Shikun Ovdim (The Workers' Housing Company) was established to provide cheap housing.

This massive machine was subsidised by external contributions. The direct and indirect support of the JNF (which paid for land leased to kibbutzim and moshavim), Joint Palestine Appeal and other institutions was vital to the Histadrut's development. It enabled the kibbutzim (never viable purely as agricultural enterprises, not least because of the cost of the lifestyles their members expected to enjoy) to exist and a bureaucratic machine which became more bloated with the years to maintain itself. Mapai's domination of the Jewish Agency from 1935, its leading role in world Zionism and, subsequently, its control of Israel's state apparatus from 1948 until 1977 (latterly as the Labour Party) enabled it to ensure that the institutions of the Zionist Labour movement received a steady flow of funds. In turn, the Histadrut provided a solid base of support for Mapai, backing its policies towards the Yishuv as a whole, the Arabs and the British.

The biggest employer of labour in Palestine during the Mandate years was the government. Britain's policy initially was to recruit employees from the Arab and Jewish communities roughly according to their proportions within the population. Later, it was persuaded to adopt a new concept of 'fairness' in employment: taking on workers according to the proportion of tax revenue which their communities provided to the government. The more developed Jewish economy delivered more taxes, and so this meant tilting recruitment towards Jews. The Histadrut consistently sought to persuade the government to hire more Jews and its companies sought government contracts to provide more work for Jews. Successes were limited, until Britain found itself under pressure during the 1936–39 Arab revolt and, especially, during the Second World War, when Solel Boneh handled contracts for the Allies throughout the Middle East, incidentally offering a convenient cover for contacts with Zionist groups in Arab countries. The war, in fact, was when the Jewish labour economy really took off, helped by contracts to supply goods to Britain.[38]

The Histadrut's competence extended to military affairs. Before the First World War, a defence organisation known as 'Hashomer' (The Watchman) had been formed. Its members took on the responsibility of defending Jewish settlements, replacing Arab watchmen, who were regarded as unreliable. When the first large scale attacks by Arabs on Jews took place in 1920, Hashomer proved unequal to the challenge. It was disbanded in May 1920 and, a month later, replaced by a new organisation, the Haganah ('Defence'). Shortly afterwards, it was placed under the authority of the Histadrut.[39]

At first, the Haganah was small, poorly trained and ill-equipped. Only after the 1929 disturbances, when the Yishuv had to rely on British forces to defend Jewish communities, did it feel sufficiently shaken to put its weight behind the Haganah. (Its later rivals, the Irgun Zvai Leumi and LEHI, commanded much less support and were far smaller.) Soon, the Haganah had set up an effective arms procurement organisation to bring in weaponry purchased in Europe and it went on to organise an underground arms industry which could produce grenades, bombs and cartridges.

During the 1936–39 revolt, a hard-pressed Britain agreed to the formation of the Settlement Police, to be paid by the Jewish Agency. Through this force, which had the duty of defending Jewish settlements, thousands of Jews were able to be trained legally in the use of firearms and serve in a disciplined structure. Many Haganah members joined the Settlement Police, so strengthening the Haganah itself. This force:

> reached its peak at the beginning of 1939, when it was reorganised into ten territorial battalions. In total, it encompassed some 22,000 members, or about five per cent of the Yishuv, with somewhere around 8000 rifles at their disposal. The Haganah had at the peak of the disturbances only 6000 rifles, 24 machine guns and 600 medium and submachine guns.[40]

Courtesy of Britain, the Haganah at this time had the invaluable assistance of Orde Wingate, best known now for organising the Chindits, who operated behind Japanese lines in Burma during the Second World War. A devout Christian who regarded Jewish settlement in Palestine as the fulfilment of Biblical prophecy, he became an ardent Zionist. While serving as a captain in Palestine in 1936, he persuaded the British command to let him train Haganah units to fight armed Arab groups. These were the Special Night Squads, whose operations were concentrated on defending the British oil pipeline which crossed the Galilee and terminated at Haifa. Wingate instilled an offensive spirit (as well as ruthlessness) in his troops and encouraged the Haganah to see the importance of taking the initiative and striking at its enemies on terms of its own choosing, rather than maintaining a passive defensive posture.

During the Second World War, 28,000 men and 4000 women of the Yishuv served in the British army, among them Moshe Dayan, who lost an eye in the campaign against the Vichy forces in Syria in 1941. These volunteers and other Jewish veterans who came to Palestine following the war brought invaluable skills and experience to the Haganah. By spring 1947, the Haganah had a strength of 46,000; Ben Gurion was informed on 1 May 1948 that it had a fighting force of 22,425 ready for action, a number which rose to 35,368 by 4 June.[41] Their shortage of weapons was significantly eased by the Czechoslovak arms deal of January 1948. Twelve days before the State of Israel was proclaimed, the Haganah was taken from the official control of the Histadrut, to be transformed into the Israeli army.

There were others besides the mainstream labour Zionists who struggled for the creation of a Jewish state – notably the rightist Revisionists and the Marxist-Zionists of Hashomer Hatzair – but it is clear who played the main role. The major institutions of labour Zionism – Mapai and the Histadrut – were central to a web of relationships, institutional and personal, which by the mid-1930s meshed together the Jewish Agency, World Zionist Organisation, JNF, kibbutzim, moshavim and the Haganah. Hashomer Hatzair was tied into this network in spite of its endeavours to preserve its independence; the Revisionists' attempts to build alternatives had limited success. The network dominated by Mapai only began to disintegrate after the Revisionists' heirs in the Likud party won office in 1977 and squeezed the subsidies which had kept it functioning inefficiently for decades.

In the 30 years of British rule, Zionism created a state in waiting. All the elements which would be needed to establish Jewish sovereignty over most of the land of Palestine were already in place at the beginning of the 1940s.

The Palestinian Arab Revolt

The Palestinian Arabs' struggle to frustrate Zionist ambitions in Palestine was hampered by the factors already outlined. Their society was ill adapted to confront a determined movement of European colonisation. Its social relations and economic structure made it vulnerable to the threat it now faced. Not only did it lack equivalents to Mapai, the Histadrut or the Haganah, but it did not see the need to match them or have any concept of how to do so: what they represented came from outside Palestinian Arab political culture. This meant that the Palestinians were unable to make full use of the strengths which they did possess vis-a-vis the Zionists: numerical preponderance, demographic domination of the bulk of the countryside and interior and familiarity with the land.

In spite of Britain's commitment to the Balfour Declaration, Palestinian Arab leaders hoped to persuade it that their opposition to Zionism was justified: Britain should take account of their fears for the future and halt the growth of Zionist settlement in Palestine. This was the hope of most of their people too. Only in the mid-1930s, on the eve of the Great Revolt, did anti-British feeling become pronounced. By then, the great majority of the Palestinian Arabs had come to recognise, through bitter experience, that Britain was the principal guarantor of the Zionist enterprise in Palestine.

When the revolt broke out in 1936, it became a struggle against Britain as well as Zionism. Haj Amin al-Husseini, Mufti of Jerusalem and the most influential Palestinian Arab leader, finally felt obliged to adopt the stand taken by the mass movement of his people; most of his rivals did not do so even then, still hoping for a change of heart on Britain's part. The attitude of the Palestinian Arab leaders towards Britain was conditioned by the power relationship between them: having recognised that Britain was firmly in control of their country, they adapted to that reality, feeling that they were bound to lose a head-on confrontation with it. Britain, for its part, tried, as far as possible, to avoid appearing to impose its will by sheer force. It sought to secure the co-operation of Palestinian Arab leaders through consultation, but also (as the Ottoman rulers had done) through the subtle exploitation of differences between them. In 1920, for example, after dismissing Musa Qassem al-Husseini as mayor of Jerusalem for his forceful anti-Zionist stand, it appointed Ragheb al-Nashashibi, a lifelong rival of the Husseinis, to the post. In 1921, however, the British interfered in the election for the post of Mufti of Jerusalem to ensure that it went to Haj Amin al-Husseini, although he did not gain the highest vote. The British authorities saw him as a moderate and influential person whose co-operation would be of value and indeed, until after the outbreak of the Great Revolt, he tended to exercise a restraining influence on the more violent manifestations of Palestinian Arab feeling towards the Jews and had persistently tried to influence British policies by peaceful persuasion. Britain had certain means by which it could exert pressure on Arab leaders appointed to official posts in Palestine, short of threatening their dismissal. In the case of the Mufti, it paid his salary as head of the Supreme Muslim Council.

When violent opposition to Zionism erupted, it was a spontaneous, grassroots expression of feeling, not inspired by the established leaders. In 1921, clashes between rival Jewish communist and social-democratic May Day demonstrations in Jaffa were the trigger for attacks by local Arabs on any Jews found in the area. In August 1929, following a period of rising tension, clashes broke out over attempts by Jewish militants to strengthen the Jewish position at the Western Wall in Jerusalem. A demonstration by the Revisionists was followed by Arab riots. Jews were attacked not only in Jerusalem, but elsewhere too, most notoriously in Hebron, where 64 members of the city's ancient Jewish community were slaughtered. This community was religious and lived in peace with its neighbours; it did not support Zionism.

The attack on Hebron's Jews, although carried out in one of the most socially conservative parts of Palestine, reveals the limitations within which much popular Palestinian understanding of the conflict with Zionism was constrained. The notions of collective responsibility which had exerted a powerful influence in the relations between clans and in the regulation of female behaviour were easily transferred to a new context: that of the national struggle in Palestine. The Hebron Jews fell victim to Palestinian Arab violence because they were identified as belonging to the same entity as the Arabs' Zionist enemies and they were vulnerable.[42] Quite apart from ethical considerations, acting towards Jews in Palestine as though they were collectively responsible for what particular Jews did could only be counter-productive for the Palestinian Arabs, promoting as it did the consolidation of the separate Jewish society being built by Zionism.

The Revolt Begins

The most determined and sustained challenge to the Zionist project in Palestine prior to the Intifada was the Great Revolt. It lasted for nearly three years, from 1936 to 1939. The underlying factors behind it were the sharp increase in Jewish immigration to Palestine following the rise of the Nazis to power in Germany and the growth of popular recognition that the Palestinian leaders had failed to secure British agreement to their demands. Militant opposition to Zionism coalesced outside the organisations controlled by the established leadership, in bodies such as the Istiqlal Party, nationalist Boy Scouts, Young Men's Muslim Associations and the Congress of Youth. Among them, there was a widespread conviction that only violent action could now bring Arab Palestine the realisation of its objectives.

Particularly significant was the movement led by Izz al-Din al-Qassam, of the Haifa Young Men's Muslim Association. Al-Qassam was born in Syria and studied at Cairo's Al-Azhar University. He was a devout Muslim. Sentenced to death by the French for his participation in Syrian resistance to their rule, he came to Haifa in 1921. His work was concentrated among the poor who came to the city to seek employment, often after being forced off their land by indebtedness or Zionist land acquisition. Slowly and patiently, al-Qassam worked to create an underground movement, inculcated with a revolutionary spirit, which he hoped would become the spearhead of an armed popular revolt. In November 1935, al-Qassam and a small group of followers encountered and killed a police sergeant in the hill country south-west of Haifa. British forces pursued them and they were cornered on 21 November near Ya'abad. Al-Qassam called upon his men to 'Die like martyrs!' He and four others did so; the rest were captured. Though prematurely exposed to its enemies, the movement which al-Qassam led proved its worth: his followers were prominent among the local leaders of the Great Revolt.[43]

The established leaders did not like the fact that al-Qassam had acted independently, nor did they welcome the militant opposition to Zionism and Britain which he encouraged: they still hoped to convince Britain to change its policies by peaceful persuasion. None of them came to al-Qassam's funeral.

Al-Qassam has been an inspiration to modern Palestinian resistance organisations, although each has chosen to stress those aspects of his views and activities which appeared to validate their own political perspectives. Ghassan Kanafani of the PFLP emphasised al-Qassam's determination to build a revolutionary organisation among the poorer sectors of the people, with a firm stand against British imperialism as well as Zionism; Hamas has stressed the centrality of his faith as a Muslim to his ideas and Islam as the motivating force of his movement's activists.[44] The record of al-Qassam's movement indicates that resistance could best be mobilised and sustained by a highly motivated revolutionary organisation, based among those with the strongest reasons to fight. It was not a lesson that the leadership of the Palestinian Arab national movement was prepared to learn.

A few months after al-Qassam's death, in April 1936, a series of violent incidents led the government to impose a State of Emergency throughout Palestine. Arab reaction was swift. Strikes declared in Nablus and Jerusalem spread to the rest of the country. A network of National Committees sprang up to organise the protest movement.[45] Ex-Istiqlal members called for elections to be organised to constitute a leadership, whether through convening a national congress or **through** a meeting of the representatives of the National Committees, but the established leaders had no intention of yielding their place to more revolutionary elements.They had been overtaken by events, but hurried forward to put themselves in charge. After some hesitation, for fear of provoking British anger, they established the Arab Higher Committee (AHC) on 25 April, whose membership was constituted without elections. Haj Amin al-Husseini was president, and its other members were the leaders of the Arab political parties, two Istiqlalists, and two Christian leaders drawn from the Arab parties. The AHC decided that the strike should continue until the British met the Palestinian Arab demands.

The strike lasted for six months. The British refused to negotiate while it continued and had a number of means to hand with which to blunt its impact. Their most valuable ally was the Jewish population, who naturally carried on working. The Zionist leadership saw the opportunities that now presented themselves and took them. When there was a chance for Jews to replace striking Arabs, they took it, and Jewish workers were prepared, when working alongside Arabs, to put in more time and effort when the latter struck. As a result, the port of Haifa, with its mixed labour force, went on working because it was not possible to bring out the Arab workers on a protracted and effective strike. The workforce in the port of Jaffa was completely Arab and mounted a total strike, but Ben Gurion recognised how this could be turned to the advantage of the Zionists: the Yishuv leadership secured British permission to build a wharf at Tel Aviv and so took the first step to create a port which would soon overshadow Jaffa. Most industry was Jewish-owned. Jewish firms which still employed Arabs or bought materials from Arab sources now turned to the Jewish sector or overseas suppliers to meet their needs.

Calls to extend the strike to Arabs in government employment were made by the Mufti's rivals, including Ragheb al-Nashashibi, who knew full well that this would put him in a difficult position, as a public employee himself. In the event, the public sector was not called out. In such circumstances, the British were able to sit out the strike. The AHC had sought support for the Palestinians from the Arab states, which it hoped would use their influence to persuade Britain to alter its policy. In September, it discreetly appealed to the Arab rulers to call for an end to the strike and disorders, which they did the following month. The AHC was then able to endorse the call, as if in response to an Arab initiative, thus saving face.

There was, in fact, little point in continuing the strike. British and Zionist counter-measures had proved effective in containing its impact. Palestinian Arabs were losing their livelihoods to no obvious advantage: small wonder that they had no hesitation in heeding the call to resume work.

An armed resistance movement began to operate during the strike. Random attacks against isolated Jews – travellers or people living in exposed locations – began to give way in May 1936 to more organised violence by armed bands. These included groups belonging to al-Jihad al-Muqaddas (Holy War), led by Abd al-Qadir al-Husseini and aligned with the Mufti, and other armed bodies too. At first, their attacks focused on the roads, railways and cities, but British counter-measures in urban areas were ruthless and effective. Jaffa, a stronghold of Palestinian nationalism, contained an Old City with a warren of small streets and alleys into which armed activists could escape following attacks. Claiming to be acting for public health reasons, the government demolished the homes of 6000 people in July, allowing easier military access to the city. British repression was only effective in the cities and towns: the strength of the armed groups in the countryside remained undiminished when the AHC called upon them to cease operations at the end of the strike.

Britain appointed a Royal Commission under Lord Peel to investigate the causes of the unrest in Palestine. On the day it set out for Palestine, Britain announced that it would not suspend Jewish immigration while the commission conducted its investigations: there would be no face-saving concessions to the AHC. In protest, the AHC boycotted the commission's investigations, but rescinded its decision following criticism from Arab heads of state. This was just in time to allow it to make an inadequately prepared presentation of the Arab case to the commission in the last week of its three months in Palestine: it contrasted very unfavourably with the polished testimonies of British and Zionist spokesmen.

This incident was not the last of its kind: futile gestures made without serious consideration of the tactics most appropriate to each concrete situation have littered the history of the Palestinian national movement. On this occasion, most Palestinian Arabs felt aggrieved by the British government's attitude and thought the AHC's decision justified. A more imaginative leadership might nevertheless have taken another course. At a time when popular protest had been halted, the leadership would not have undermined a mass movement by testifying to the commission. It would have avoided appearing inflexible to the outside world and might have gained some political ground by delivering a well-considered presentation of its case. Ultimately, the boycott made it appear extreme to the Western world and its climbdown made it also seem weak.

Made public on 7 July 1937, the Peel Commission's report recommended that Palestine be partitioned. The north-central coastal region and the Galilee would become a Jewish state. Britain would continue to administer the Jerusalem-Bethlehem area, plus a corridor linking it to the coast. The remaining area would be united with Transjordan. Ben Gurion and his colleagues declared their acceptance of the recommendations, with qualifications; the Arab leadership rejected what they saw as the vivisection of their homeland.

The Arab revolt re-ignited at the end of September, with the assassination of the British District Commissioner for Galilee. Its second phase differed markedly from the first. The revolt was now primarily a rural movement, the backbone of which was the peasantry, the largest sector of the Palestinian Arab people. They provided its fighters, furnished them with food and information and sheltered them. The rebels took control of the hill regions of Palestine, from Hebron up to Galilee, as well as the purely Arab lowlands of the Gaza and Beersheba regions. They collected taxes and set up their own courts. British rule contracted to the major towns and the largely Jewish areas. The revolt reached the peak of its success in the autumn of 1938, symbolised by its liberation of the Old City of Jerusalem in October. Thereafter, it went into rapid decline, finally fizzling out in the summer of 1939.

The main reason for its defeat was that the forces ranged against the Palestinian Arabs were too strong for them. Britain was prepared to commit the resources required to suppress the revolt, sending 20,000 troops for that purpose. Unlike Arab nationalists who had revolted against colonial rule in Egypt, Syria and other countries, the Palestinians faced Zionism, as well as a European colonial state. When the revolt began, the Yishuv was already a viable society, able to cope with the Arabs' strike and boycott of the Jewish economy. This community was more than happy to help the British keep communications functioning and to assist the suppression of Arab resistance.

The revolt was weakened by internal factors. Its leaders' qualities never matched the people's courage and determination. They lagged behind the popular movement at the outset and after a first show of unity, their ingrained factionalism soon reasserted itself. The Nashashibi-led faction tended to look for an accommodation with Britain, using the assistance of Abdullah and other Arab leaders, while the Mufti and his allies took a more determined stand and at the same time sought to impose their control on the popular movement. The Mufti's quest for a monopoly of power in Palestinian Arab society led him to use violence against his rivals, pushing them towards an accommodation with the British.

This contest did not take place in a vacuum: old habits of organising, existing regional and clan differences combined with factional rivalries to ensure that the various armed Palestinian groups were not brought together into a single national liberation army. In the second phase of the revolt, overall leadership of the armed groups was claimed by the Iraqi, Fawzi al-Qawukji, who arrived with Arab volunteers in August 1936 and won the support of six of the groups' commanders. It was also claimed by the Arab Higher Committee, now forced to base itself in Damascus and firmly under the Mufti's control. There was no integrated command structure, no mechanism for rapidly concentrating forces where they were most needed and no means for developing a strategy to take the struggle forward. The armed groups operated independently of each other and were liable to be picked off by British operations. Being composed mainly of individuals from the localities where they operated, they knew the lie of the land well, which was an advantage, but they also gave expression to existing conflicts within Palestinian society which were exacerbated under the stress of an arduous protracted struggle. There were people who would rather stand aloof from the revolt than join forces with members of a rival clan.

The trial and execution of individuals accused of collaboration by the armed bands was sometimes a means of settling old scores. Even when it was not, what was gained by removing one set of the enemy's eyes and ears in a community could be more than cancelled out by his family and clan being antagonised. 'Peace bands' – armed groups which opposed the rebels – emerged as a result and the ferocity of the rebel response only contributed to the alienation of larger numbers of people.[46]

The Palestinians justly remember the 1936–39 revolt as a heroic episode in their history and a high point in their struggle. They sustained a prolonged fight against the might of Britain and the Zionist Jewish community. The revolt's strength came from popular mobilisation, when the mass of the Palestinian Arab people acted, largely autonomously of their established leaders, for a cause which they believed to be wholly just. Zionists in the Western labour movement attempted to portray Arab opposition to Zionism as the work of reactionary 'effendis' inciting a gullible and ignorant people against an enlightened Jewish community whose progressive example, they feared, might seduce the masses into turning against their Arab oppressors. This was sheer fiction. It was precisely the poorest sections of the Palestinian people who gave and endured the most during the revolt. The impetus for this sustained struggle came from below, not from the 'effendis', and the rebels acted out of the knowledge that Zionism was a real threat, not out of ignorance or bigotry.

The revolt cost about 5000 killed and 15,000 wounded out of a population of a million Palestinian Arabs. The British lost 101 dead and the Jews, 463.[47] The losses they suffered, the internal conflicts which were exacerbated during this struggle and the impact of the ultimate outcome of their revolt on their morale left the Palestinians ill-placed to face the next crisis when it came eight years later.

What would happen then was foreshadowed by the Peel Commission's report. Its proposals were an implicit admission that the provisions of the Mandate could not be honoured and that Britain had chosen to keep its commitment to support the establishment of a Jewish National Home in Palestine in preference to respecting the rights of the Palestinian Arabs. Partition was put on the political agenda for Palestine for the first time; as already mentioned, this led to a shift in Zionist colonisation strategy. A claim to expanded borders would be made through the establishment of Jewish settlements in areas regarded as vital to a Jewish state and in which there was no existing Jewish population. The report's proposal to 'transfer' unwanted minority populations from each of the two major regions primarily meant the removal of Arabs, by compulsion if necessary, from the Galilee and northern coastal region, where they made up the majority of the population, as no viable Jewish state could be established in Palestine otherwise. Only a few thousand Jews lived in the area designated for the Arabs. While the idea of 'transfer' was not new, the Peel Commission's proposals served to legitimate it.

During the revolt, the Palestinian Arabs relied mainly upon their own resources, but the Arab states had been drawn into active intervention in the conflict, as well as into inter-Arab politics in Palestine, with mixed consequences for the future. They had intervened at the request of the AHC in 1936 to bring the revolt to a temporary halt and they have been involved ever since. There was a tendency for the Palestinian Arab leadership to become increasingly dependent on the Arab states, especially once

Britain had banned the AHC, forcing it to make Damascus its official headquarters. The Arab states tried to achieve a unified public political stand towards Britain and Zionism, but they were pursuing divergent interests: Abdullah of Transjordan coveted Palestine and so shared an interest with Britain and the Zionists in frustrating the emergence of an independent Arab state there, which would have been dominated by the Mufti and his supporters.[48] Egypt, Syria and Saudi Arabia were wary of Abdullah's ambitions and were thus ready to back the AHC fully. The increased Arab state role in the Palestine conflict was signalled by their participation in the St James conference.

After the Revolt

By autumn 1938, as the threat of war with Germany loomed larger, Britain was ready to drop its support for partition and go some way towards meeting Palestinian Arab concerns as the price of keeping the Arab world quiet. The St James conference was officially convened in London on 7 February 1939 as an Arab–Jewish meeting to find a solution to the Palestine question. It was attended by representatives from Egypt, Iraq, Saudi Arabia, Transjordan and Yemen as well as Palestinian Arab and Jewish delegations, although the Arab and Jewish delegations did not meet face to face. Britain hoped that the Arab states' delegations would press the Palestinian Arab representatives to modify their demands. In the event, they proved unbending, insisting that they wanted independence for Palestine without delay and an end to Jewish immigration and the 'National Home' policy. No agreement was possible.

Following the failure of the St James conference, Britain issued the MacDonald White Paper on 17 May 1939. It appeared to represent an Arab victory. The British government declared that it was not part of its policy that Palestine should become a Jewish state. It imposed apparently strict limits on land sales to Jews and put a ceiling on the number of further Jewish immigrants who were to be admitted to Palestine: 75,000 would be allowed to enter over the next five years, after which any more could only come with Arab consent. The White Paper called for self-governing institutions to be developed in preparation for Palestinian independence within ten years. The AHC, still insistent that its demands be met in full, foolishly rejected the White Paper out of hand. Yet there is no doubt that it marked a significant shift in Britain's official position.

The Zionists recognised as much. The cry of 'appeasement' went up. Britain's concessions to a people seeking to retain possession of their homeland were equated with those it made to totalitarian dictators engaged in territorial aggrandisement. This marked a turning point in Britain's relationship with the Zionist movement, which believed that the implementation of the White Paper policy would frustrate the realisation of its dream of a Jewish state. The Zionists resolved to fight the White Paper policy – in the case of the Irgun Zvai Leumi, with arms – but events in Palestine were overtaken by the Second World War. For the vast majority of the Yishuv, it was clear that, in a war which ranged Britain against Nazi Germany, the Jews of Palestine had to side with Britain, as much as they detested its new Palestine policy. Only a small group led by Abraham Stern, which split from the Irgun, disagreed and saw Britain as its main enemy.[49] The Yishuv participated in the war effort against Nazi Germany but, like the political leaders of the Allied powers, those of the Yishuv simultaneously prepared for the post-war world.

In May 1942, around 600 delegates from Palestine, America and Europe gathered at New York's Biltmore Hotel. They came for an 'extraordinary Zionist conference', not a Zionist congress; nevertheless, this meeting carried much weight, both because of the breadth of representation there and because of David Ben Gurion's participation . It adopted a statement which became known as the Biltmore Programme. This called for the establishment of a 'Jewish Commonwealth' in Palestine – essentially, a Jewish state – and for Palestine to be opened up to unrestricted Jewish immigration, under the control of the Jewish Agency.

The conference at the Biltmore reflected a shift which was taking place in the strategy of the Zionist leadership. It refocused its efforts at an international level on winning and consolidating the backing of the country which was set to emerge as the strongest power in the world – the United States. Britain continued to be the target of lobbying and pressure, as the power in control in Palestine, but it would be the support of the US which would count for most.

The Nazi attempt to annihilate Europe's Jews during the Second World War caused a decisive change in Jewish attitudes towards Zionism, as well as influencing how non-Jews perceived the Palestine conflict. Zionist arguments about the need for the Jews to have a state of their own appeared to have been vindicated. At the end of the war, public sympathy for the Jews in the non-colonial world was translated into endorsement of what was presented as the dearest aspiration of Jews everywhere: statehood in Palestine. British attempts to curb illegal immigration were easily pilloried as callous and perverse actions against a people who had already suffered unequalled horrors. In this atmosphere, few were ready to spare a thought for the Palestinian Arabs and their rights. In any case, who was to speak for them? Haj Amin al-Husseini had fled to Germany during the war. Reasoning that his enemy's enemy was his friend, he rested his hopes of preventing the creation of a Jewish state in Palestine on a German victory. Following Hitler's defeat, the Mufti could still meet Arab politicians and heads of state as the leader of the Palestinian Arabs, but it is hardly surprising that none of the victorious allied powers, East or West, wanted to have any political dealings with him.

Following the war, Britain wished to escape from its increasingly messy entanglement in Palestine and put its fate in the hands of the United Nations (UN). The special commission established by the UN to prepare recommendations on Palestine's future was divided. A minority proposed that Palestine should become independent as a unified state. The majority supported a plan for the partition of Palestine into Arab and Jewish states, linked in an economic union. Although Jews made up only one in three of Palestine's population, the Jewish state was to have 56 per cent of Palestine's territory – most of which was in Arab hands. An enclave containing Jerusalem and Bethlehem would be placed under an international administration and the remainder of the land was to become a Palestinian Arab state.

The UN General Assembly considered the proposals in November 1947. This was a UN in which much of the world was unrepresented. Large parts of Asia and Africa were still under European rule. Their experiences had given them a different perspective on movements of European colonisation in 'backward' countries than that prevalent in the West, but they had no voice in the decision before the UN. A two-thirds majority of UN member states was needed to approve Resolution 181, in favour of partition. The USA and USSR both supported it, Soviet-aligned states followed the Kremlin line obediently and the USA brought pressure to bear on six vulnerable states to reverse their stated positions and support partition. This secured the votes of Haiti, Liberia and the Philippines – enough to provide the requisite majority.

The Jewish Agency officially accepted the partition plan. Ben Gurion saw it as offering international endorsement of a Jewish state as well as providing a territory from which it could expand as opportunity permitted. The Palestinian Arabs rejected the plan, believing it to be wrong in principle (they saw themselves as the rightful possessors of the land and did not want their country to be divided) and doubly unjust in its allocation of most of the land to the minority population.

It has often been argued that the Palestinian Arabs should have accepted partition in 1947, so that they could at least have salvaged some 40 per cent of their homeland. Such 'moderation' might have won them a public relations point, but there was no guarantee that either the Zionist leadership in Palestine or indeed the leaders of the surrounding Arab states would have respected the independence and territorial integrity of a Palestinian Arab state. In fact, understandings had already been reached between the Jewish Agency and Amir Abdullah of Transjordan to frustrate the foundation of a Palestinian Arab state and give a large swathe of its central area to Transjordan. There is no doubt who intended to inherit the rest.

Following the UN's endorsement of the partition plan, the Palestinian Arabs again took to arms, but gave no indication that they had drawn lessons from the 1936–39 revolt. They had not used the intervening years to train a disciplined national force of fighters, collect intelligence and formulate detailed military plans. Armed Palestinian groups concentrated on bomb attacks, sniping at Jewish neighbourhoods and ambushing Jewish traffic on the roads. The latter activity stretched the resources of the Haganah and, in particular, placed the Jewish part of Jerusalem under siege, but the overall impact of Palestinian Arab armed actions was limited in the absence of an effective strategy and the material resources to significantly damage Zionist military capabilities. The war of the roads could have contributed to an Arab victory in conditions in which the odds had been more even and attacks by locally-based fighters supplemented offensives by larger, quasi-regular formations aimed at destroying enemy military power. This did not happen. The Arab Liberation Army of volunteers from the Arab countries, led by Fawzi al-Qawukji, carried out a few ill-planned and poorly executed attacks, with little co-ordination with Palestinian Arab forces.[50]

Between November 1947 and 14 May 1948, when the British withdrew, the Haganah grew in strength and succeeded in holding almost all the Jewish population centres in Palestine: only the Etzion bloc, near Hebron, and four isolated settlements in the Jerusalem area fell to its foes or were relinquished. The Haganah mainly stood on the defensive in the first months of the conflict, but even then, it did not limit itself to passive defence, launching tactical offensives in response to Arab actions and to consolidate its own position. In April 1948, it went on to the attack. It was well placed to do so. It had over 60,000 men under arms, organised in nine brigades, as well as an elite strike force, the Palmach. It was well trained and led, with an efficient supply system. While the Irgun and LEHI armed forces were not at the Haganah's disposal, their independent actions at least served to dissipate Arab strength.[51]

The Haganah clearly demonstrated its superiority over the Arab forces in the series of operations which commenced at the beginning of April. Its main reason for not going on to the strategic offensive earlier was that it wished to avoid a direct confrontation with the British army, not because it doubted its ability to defeat the Palestinians. It was believed that, by waiting to launch large scale offensive operations until a month and a half before the end of the Mandate, the Haganah could reduce the likelihood of a strong British response. It implemented Plan Dalet. Its aim was:

> To gain control of the area allotted to the Jewish State and defend its borders, and those of the blocs of Jewish settlements and such Jewish population as were outside those borders, against a regular or pararegular enemy operating from bases outside or inside the area of the Jewish State.[52]

The 13 operations envisaged under Plan Dalet were intended to consolidate the blocs of territory under Haganah control, open up communication lines between them and block the avenues of approach to the more densely populated Jewish areas by regular Arab forces, whose intervention following British withdrawal was expected. The Haganah hoped to prevail over its enemies by remaining on the defensive in most parts of the country and concentrating strong forces to execute carefully planned offensive operations in key areas.

The distinguished Palestinian professor, Walid Khalidi, saw in Plan Dalet a blueprint for the expulsion of the Palestinian Arabs from the territory which would be incorporated into the Jewish state, and other Palestinian writers have largely shared that view.[53] Conventional Israeli scholarship claimed that it was formulated with purely military objectives in mind.[54] For what it's worth, this writer's view is that the security situation of the Yishuv in spring 1948 was such that there is good reason to believe that the primary objectives of Plan Dalet were strictly military and the initial expulsions of Palestinian Arabs can be explained chiefly by operational considerations (above all, the removal of hostile populations who harboured or were believed to harbour fighters from areas adjacent to Jewish communication routes), but that, in the conflicts of 1948 as a whole, a clear trend is discernible: as the Haganah (and then the Israeli army) grew in confidence, the expulsion of the unwanted Arab population became a more and more important objective in its own right.

Most of the objectives of Plan Dalet were achieved. Its execution and that of subsequent Israeli military operations stands in sharp contrast to the Palestinian Arabs' military performance. Numerically inferior in fighters, disorganised, with inadequate weaponry and finances and poor political leadership, their resistance buckled under the Zionist hammerblows.

With the end of the British Mandate, the independence of the State of Israel was proclaimed in Tel Aviv on 14 May. Units of the Lebanese, Syrian, Iraqi, Transjordanian and Egyptian armies crossed the borders of Palestine, supposedly to help the Palestinian Arabs, but they differed in their objectives and failed to co-ordinate their operations: the nominal overall commander was unable to make them work together. The 1948–49 Arab–Israeli War unfolded in phases of fighting separated by ceasefires; it was only in the first, from 15 May to 11 June, that the combined Arab forces seriously strained the Israeli defences; thereafter, Israel held the initiative and defeated its enemies piecemeal, in the process enlarging the area under its control to just under 80 per cent of Palestine.

In 1948, the Palestinians suffered more than a battlefield defeat. Their society was overwhelmed by that built by the Zionist movement. The Palestinian Arabs and the Arab states did not use the resources they had to the best advantage, but that was not the main reason for their defeat. They were at war with economic, social and administrative structures, an education system and political culture which they were not able to match, and from which their enemy's armed forces drew most of their resources. Israel's support from external sources was more limited than in later wars: this conflict, more than those, testified to the importance of its own strengths to its victory.

Facing a stronger enemy and already stressed by the foregoing conflicts, Palestinian society crumbled under the impact of intensified strife. At the end of 1947, a steady exodus of richer Palestinians from areas on the front line of the conflict began, depriving communities of those to whom they looked for leadership. As village after village fell to the Zionist military forces from mid-February 1948 onwards, more and more Palestinians fled. Expulsion at gunpoint, threats, massacres and fear of massacres were the main reasons for their flight, but other factors influencing the Palestinian Arabs' judgement included the disorientation of many urban communities following the departure of their leaders and their fears about how their enemies would treat their womenfolk. Demoralisation worsened matters, as first the Palestinian Arabs' own fighters were overwhelmed and then the Arab armies were defeated.

The Palestinians who fled left believing that they would soon return. In earlier times, people had left their homes at times of danger and returned when it was safe to do so. In 1948, many Palestinians locked the doors of their homes and took their keys with them, confident that, in a matter of weeks or months, the fighting would end and they would return. But it was not to be. Israel, having effected the 'transfer' of the great majority of an unwanted Arab population, had no intention that they should ever return. Most of the 385 or more villages the Palestinians left were destroyed. Others were settled by Jewish newcomers and renamed. Well over half of the Palestinian Arab people had been consigned to perpetual exile from their homes by Israel. In spite of all they had feared from Zionism from their first knowledge of it, they found it hard to believe that such a wrong could have been done to them.

2

A New Nation-State

In 1948, the state-in-waiting built during the years of the British Mandate became a state in being. Israel's first decade was a time of rapid change, when its population soared, its economy expanded and all aspects of life seemed to be infused with the vigour of a young, dynamic, self-confident country. This was a time of myth creation, when awkward questions about the recent past were not asked and the people appeared to be united in a common cause after the ordeal and triumph of 1948. The reality, for those who were not Jews of European origin, was less rosy, yet many would look back on it as something of a less complicated, more idealistic and hopeful period.

Thereafter, new immigration slumped. In the mid-1960s, there was an economic recession, accompanied by a wave of strikes. Israel may have been on its way to becoming a state like other states by this time, but the June 1967 war precluded that from happening. Israel occupied the West Bank and Gaza Strip (as well as Egypt's Sinai Peninsula and Syria's Golan Heights), along with the great majority of their population. The occupation intensified the conflict between Israel and the Arab world, which sought to reverse the Israeli conquests. Israel annexed East Jerusalem, but not the remaining Palestinian territories. To have done so would have threatened its Jewish character: if the Palestinians of the West Bank and Gaza Strip had become citizens with equal rights, they would have wielded considerable power in Israel's political system, but to incorporate these territories and deny their inhabitants the rights of citizenship would have created a system which the world already knew by the name of apartheid. A third option would have been to expel the Palestinians and then take the land, but immediate post-war efforts to encourage them to depart en masse eventually withered away, leaving a million and a half Palestinians who were determined to stay.

The result was that the West Bank and Gaza Strip remained under military occupation and were not formally annexed, although Israeli maps immediately ceased to show borders of any kind between them and Israel. Soldiers performed regular tours of duty there, seeking to exercise control over a population which they knew detested their presence. The West Bank and Gaza Strip quickly became a source of cheap labour for the Israeli economy, whether as providers of migrant workers or as sites of sub-contracting firms – particularly in the textiles industry. Jewish settlements were constructed in the newly-occupied areas, at first, mainly in the more sparsely populated and strategically important regions (especially the Jordan valley and around East Jerusalem), but later, following the Likud electoral victory in 1977, in the heart of the West Bank. The settlers retained all the rights of Israeli citizens while living amidst a population deprived of similar rights.

The occupation's impact on Israel was corrupting in every way. Lies had to be told about Israel's security needs and the benefits which Israeli rule was bringing to the Palestinians. The law was perverted to justify collective punishments, torture and the theft of land from the occupied population. Power over the ruled combined with fear of their resistance (always rationalised by Israeli chauvinists as motivated by Arab/Muslim hatred of Jews) to feed racist arrogance, particularly among the settler militants, who proved capable of wielding an influence on government policies out of all proportion to their numbers. Habits developed while exercising power over occupied Palestinians were not simply left behind across the former ceasefire lines: corruption, drug dealing and violence in the family have been exacerbated by the occupation.

This is not to say that all was well in Israel before 1967. The cruelties inflicted upon the Palestinians in 1948 were far worse than those carried out in 1967 and subsequently, but almost all Israeli Jews had embraced the national mythologies about the recent past and lived with it quite comfortably. The 1967 occupation opened up a period of more intense, sustained conflict with the Palestinians and produced new tensions between the self-image of Israeli Jews and reality. Many Israelis would be forced to reassess their relationship with the Palestinians to one extent or another and a few would gain insights into that relationship which would make them more questioning of their past as well as their present.

Conditional Democracy

Israel's first elections took place at the beginning of 1949, before the 'War of Independence' was fully concluded. Mapai won the largest share of votes and seats, but not a majority. It had to seek allies to form a government. This has been the pattern after every Israeli election. Israel opted for a system of proportional representation under which no party has ever achieved a majority so that it could rule on its own.

Critics of proportional representation have pointed to Israel as an example of the negative consequences of adopting such an electoral system. It is true that it has meant that the 'winning' party has never been able to rule alone and implement all the policies upon which it stood for election, but the system also has its advantages for Israel. This is a state in which there have always been strong competing interest groups which were not simply based on class or left/right divisions as understood in the world outside. In the first decades of the state, Mapai presented itself as a socialist party and was particularly identified with the Zionist labour movement – the Histadrut, its companies and institutions especially. This movement has long been dominated by Jews of European origin. It was also determinedly non-religious. The upper levels of the official labour movement, government bodies, the state-owned economy and institutions such as the Jewish Agency and JNF formed a virtual Mapai nomenklatura, providing a large and solid core of support for Mapai, and later the Labour Party, which enabled it to play a dominant role in Israeli politics for nearly 30 years. There were other interest groups which were not part of the labour movement machine: private capitalists and farmers, shopkeepers and other small business people, who were inclined to put their support behind political groupings of the right, such as Herut, or the centre, such as it was.

Religious communities, Zionist and non-Zionist, had their own parties. Those who faced discrimination and deprivation in Israel because of their national origins – Jews from the Arab world and the surviving Palestinian Arab communities – at first did not or could not find channels through which to express their specific demands, but that changed in the 1970s, adding to the complexity of the Israeli political scene.

Israeli proportional representation, which awarded seats to parties achieving more than 1 per cent of the vote, meant that the many differing interest groups within the country could find representation within the parliamentary system. It has played an important role in mediating conflicts between them. The horse-trading which followed every election restricted the room for manoeuvre of the dominant party, with mixed results. It served to broaden the base of support of each government and give the beneficiaries of such dealings more of a vested interest in the political system, but it has also made the Israeli public increasingly sceptical about the integrity of politicians in general. If anything, as ideological differences have diminished in intensity since the 1970s and political fragmentation has grown, the deals struck have become ever more shameless.

Israel has often boasted that it is the only democracy in the Middle East and this is a claim which has helped elicit Western sympathy. Yet one basic factor must be taken into account in assessing the strength of Israel's claim and that is its relationship with the Palestinians. This is not only a matter of the status of the Arab minority in Israel, who have citizenship and the vote, but also of the Palestinians who are *not* there. Israeli democracy was made possible by the exclusion of some 700,000 Palestinian Arabs in 1948 from the lands which became the territory of the State of Israel. Had they been permitted to remain, there would have been a decisive Arab majority in the new state. It is unthinkable that, having achieved a 'Jewish state' in nearly 80 per cent of Palestine, any Zionist leadership would have allowed this Arab majority to participate freely in democratic elections and frustrate the goals for which the Zionist movement had worked so doggedly by electing an Arab-dominated anti-Zionist government.[1] The exclusion of most of the Palestinian Arabs not only enabled Israel to seize their property and settle new Jewish immigrants on their land, but allowed it to extend democratic rights to those Arabs who remained, confident that Jewish demographic strength and a broad national consensus would leave them powerless to interfere with the realisation of the state's Zionist mission. The world would rightly be sceptical of the democratic credentials of any other country whose democracy was founded upon the exclusion of a majority of the electorate from all participation in its life, but the West, at least, has been prepared to overlook this fundamental flaw in Israel's case.

The exclusion of most of the Palestinian Arabs made Israel into a democracy for Israeli Jews, in which the rights of the surviving Palestinians were essentially conditional upon their status as a relatively powerless minority. This democracy has a Supreme Court which is independent of the government, a free press and protection for freedoms such as those of assembly, speech, worship and trade union activity. Whatever its limitations and faults, Israeli parliamentary democracy has served important integrative and mediatory functions in the state which have undoubtedly been a source of strength in Israel's conflict with its Arab neighbours and with the Palestinian Arabs.

Transformations

In the wake of its victory in 1948, Israel was confident and proud. The landscape of the country was reshaped by the construction of new roads and housing developments and by the tree planting projects of the Jewish National Fund. Ambitious land reclamation schemes were undertaken, including the draining of Lake Huleh[2] and the surrounding marshes and, later, the construction of the National Water Carrier, which enabled arid land in the northern Negev to be cultivated. Industry expanded and diversified. The state invested heavily in education at all levels. Israel was recognised by the great majority of the world's non-Muslim states. It could draw strength from the support of Jews elsewhere who, whatever their feelings towards Zionism had been before the Second World War, now overwhelmingly supported Israel with enthusiasm. It became part of diaspora Jewish life, its affairs covered at length in community newspapers and its welfare the object of heartfelt concern. Feelings of identification with Israel were intensified by the appearance of a growing volume of uncritical and often adulatory literature, of which Leon Uris's work of 'faction', *Exodus*, is the best known example.[3] They reached new heights in 1967, when most Jews believed that Israel stood in danger of extinction at the hands of the Arab states and were exhilarated at its victory.

At no time did Jews migrate to Israel in greater numbers than in the early 1950s. Within less than four years of the state's creation, immigration more than doubled its Jewish population. On the eve of independence, Palestine's Jewish population had numbered approximately 600,000, but by 1967, Israel had absorbed over 1.5 million immigrants. The newcomers were taught Hebrew, provided with housing and found employment. Israel has often made unfavourable comparisons between its own record in resettling some 600,000 Jews who fled from Arab countries and the Arab states' treatment of the Palestinian Arab refugees. The comparison is not apposite. From its birth until the present day, the 'Ingathering of the Exiles' has been central to the whole philosophy of Zionism: the absorption of Jewish immigrants was a fulfilment of Israel's mission as a state. Moreover, Israel needed to increase its Jewish population to settle the land, work in its growing industries and serve in its armed forces. The Arab states surrounding Israel have been lands of net emigration for the past 150 years, at least. They did not see why they should solve a refugee problem of Israel's creation. They lacked the means to resettle Palestinian Arabs easily, whereas Israel benefited from substantial financial contributions from abroad which it could spend on immigrant absorption, as well as possessing great assets in land and houses taken from the Palestinians. Moreover, whereas Jewish immigrants to Israel either wanted to live there or felt that they had no alternative but to reconcile themselves to life there, the great majority of the Palestinian refugees did not wish to be resettled elsewhere, but to return home. Many immigrants from Europe and the USA brought skills of great value to Israel: among them were scientists, academics, musicians and a high proportion of university graduates. They helped to make Israel's nuclear programme and high technology industries possible, among other things.

While Israel's achievement in absorbing great numbers of immigrants is undeniable, so are some very significant failings which have had serious long term consequences. They also say much about the state's prevailing values. It was precisely the Oriental Jews, the vast majority of whom came from the Arab countries, whose absorption was most poorly handled.[4]

The Jews from Arab lands mostly came in large numbers within very short periods of time, in response to pressures they experienced in their countries of origin: the first and largest wave of Jewish immigration from the Arab world arrived following the 1948 war, when absorption procedures were at their most unsophisticated.[5] Their very numbers stretched the resources Israel had allocated to absorption. Most were destitute. Oriental Jews went to Israel because they felt compelled (or were compelled) to leave the lands which they regarded as 'home' and it was the only place to which most could go; Jews from the West (generally referred to as Ashkenazi Jews) mainly went there having made a choice based upon Zionist commitment, not out of fear of persecution. All these factors were bound to have an impact upon the way in which the different immigrants were treated and upon how they perceived that treatment, but they only go part of the way towards explaining the different experiences of Oriental and Ashkenazi Jews.

Israel was a state which had been established mainly by the efforts of Jews of East European origin (a background shared by many West European Jews and the great majority of American Jews). Although the Yishuv had taken Hebrew as its language, rather than Yiddish (the language most commonly spoken by pre-1948 Jewish immigrants), its culture, in the very broadest sense, was European through and through. Jews coming from Europe and North America were perceived by this society to be people 'more like us' than those who came from the Arab world, regarded as backward, ignorant and, in general, partaking of all the defects of character attributed to Arabs. (In contrast, Soviet Jews were perceived to be 'like us' when they were able to come to Israel in large numbers from 1989: the differences in attitude and treatment were noted by Oriental Jews.) If all newcomers were expected to adapt to the society which existed in Israel, there is no question whatever about which of them had the most adapting to do.

In the collective memory of Israeli Oriental Jews, the time following their arrival in Israel was nightmarish. They found themselves placed in transit camps (Jews arriving from Europe also passed through them, but were usually there for a briefer period). These ma'abarot formed a stark contrast to the homes from which they came: they had tended to be among the more prosperous elements of the population in the lands they had left, with a rich culture and social life. They found themselves treated as 'primitive', their customs, clothing and thinking in need of radical transformation.[6] In the education system, most of what their children were taught as 'Jewish history' of the previous 19 centuries was that of Ashkenazi Jews.

The general absorption procedure (until the mass immigration of Soviet Jews of the late 1980s–early 1990s) involved a period of intense preparation for settlement (including being taught Hebrew), followed by dispersal to various parts of the country, where new immigrants would be assisted to find work. Oriental Jews were dispersed, but they were not integrated into existing communities. They were not made welcome in the kibbutzim, nor did they wish to embrace the collectivist and non- or anti-religious values which prevailed there: repulsion was mutual. Moshavim proved a better proposition. Sixty-five per cent of the population of moshavim founded after 1948 were of Middle Eastern and North African origin,[7] but they still only accounted for a small proportion of the new arrivals. Most found themselves trapped in inferior quality housing, often in parts of the country remote from its core population, industrial and commercial region on the coast. They lived in poor neighbourhoods in Jerusalem; in 'development towns' such as Netivot, in the Negev, ill provided with public services and with only a limited range of low-paying jobs available, or in border towns vulnerable to attack from neighbouring Arab states, like Beit Shean, in the Jordan valley, emptied of its Palestinian inhabitants and largely repopulated by Moroccan Jews, or Kiryat Shemona, in the Galilee panhandle. They were relegated to a subordinate place in the Israeli economy – although, because they were Jews, it was above that of Arab citizens.

Oriental Jews did not passively accept what was done to them, but it was some time before spontaneous and isolated acts of protest gave way to more organised movements expressing their demands. Meanwhile, their proportion within Israel's population gradually increased, as they had larger families than other Jews: by the late 1980s, they formed about 60 per cent of Israeli Jews. In the early 1970s, the Israeli Black Panthers brought Oriental Jewish protest out on to the streets of Israel. Although this movement soon splintered and collapsed, it was successful in publicising the grievances and demands of Oriental Jews and provided a spur to longer term community action. Disaffection with the Israeli Labour establishment, which had been in control in Israel when they arrived and which had connived at their disempowerment and confinement to a second-class status led the great majority of Oriental Jews to cast their votes for parties of the Israeli right, especially Likud; their support was crucial to its electoral victory in 1977, when the years of Labour hegemony were finally brought to an end.

It would be easy to conclude from this fact that Oriental Jews are firmly on the political right, but the reality is more complicated. In the first place, their vote was as much anti-Labour as pro-Likud. Secondly, while they might support Likud's general position on how to deal with the Arab world, they are not motivated by the 'Greater Israel' ideology of Herut and would be more inclined than Likud's ideologues to compromise over issues of territorial control. Thirdly, few have gone to live in West Bank and Gaza settlements. Their future political stance will depend very much on the performance of Israeli parties in meeting their demands and very little upon ideological considerations.

In spite of certain shared interests, Oriental Jews have never formed a monolithic bloc. Their attitudes vary according to the status they have achieved in Israeli society, their religiousness and their national origin. (Many Moroccan Jews, for example, still honour Morocco's king and remember the country of their origin with affection; Jews from other Arab lands have a more negative attitude towards their former homelands and especially towards their rulers.) In the late 1980s, this was reflected in a fragmentation of the Oriental vote and particularly in the emergence of the ultra-Orthodox Shas party, which achieved a representation of ten Knesset members in the 1996 elections. Shas's base of support is the Moroccan Jewish community: its gain of four seats over the previous election was, in part, a reflection of its success in mobilising non-religious Moroccan support in addition to its religious constituency.

Jewish Religion in Israel

Herzl had envisaged the creation of a Jewish national state, in which there would be a rigorous separation between religion and the state, but this was not to be. The status accorded to the religious authorities in Jewish life by the British during the Mandate was reinforced by the government of the young State of Israel.

The Israeli government gave control over matters of marriage, divorce and burial to the religious authorities within each of the country's religious communities – in the Jewish sector, specifically to the Orthodox authorities. There has never been any provision for those who might wish to deal with such matters in civil institutions, although over 80 per cent of Israeli Jews are not religious. This means, among other things, that Jewish women wishing to obtain a divorce are dependent upon the co-operation of their husbands. It also means that marriage across religious lines for the few who want it is very difficult. The Jewish religious authorities will not marry a Jew and a non-Jew; the Muslim ones permit the marriage of a Muslim man and a Jewish woman, but not the marriage of a Muslim woman to a Jewish man. Most mixed couples who wish to wed therefore have to marry abroad in countries which do have civil marriage.

The new state also agreed that the armed forces' food should be subject to rabbinical supervision to ensure that it was kosher and that they should observe the sabbath as far as possible. Wanting to avoid a head-on clash with the Orthodox religious, Ben Gurion agreed that women who objected to performing military service on religious grounds would be exempted from doing so, as would men who were engaged in religious studies. Such gestures were also a means of giving expression to the state's 'Jewish character' and acknowledging the role of Judaism in preserving a Jewish identity over centuries of dispersal.[8]

In the first three decades of the twentieth century, religious Jews in Palestine were almost all anti-Zionist. A Zionist trend emerged after Avraham Kook (who became first Ashkenazi chief rabbi of Palestine), among others, argued that Zionism and the settlement of the Land of Israel were the signs of the beginning of the divine redemption of the Jews.[9] The chief political manifestation of religious Zionism during the Mandate period was the Mizrachi party, which became the largest constituent of Israel's National Religious Party (NRP). The NRP has been a regular participant in government coalitions. Regarded as a party of the centre until the early 1970s, it moved into the camp of the chauvinist far right thereafter, encouraged by the West Bank settler activists of Gush Emunim (Bloc of the Faithful) which was established within the NRP by religious youth. Anti-Zionist religious Jews have been divided between a large majority, who have opted to participate in the Israeli political system and Neturei Karta, who boycott it entirely. The former were chiefly represented by Agudat Israel, a party which has slowly moved away from its original strongly anti-Zionist stance.

Since the end of the 1970s, the religious vote has grown, but become more fragmented. Tehiya, now defunct, was formed by opponents of the terms of the Egyptian–Israeli peace agreement, uniting religious and non-religious opponents of any Israeli withdrawal from occupied Arab territory; United Torah Judaism was formed by Agudat Israel and Degel Hatorah, a smaller Orthodox party; Shas emerged. Religious parties have commanded close to 20 per cent of the Israeli vote in the 1990s, which suggests that they are securing practically all the votes of the religious communities.

These parties have had two main objectives which they have pursued through negotiating terms with the dominant secular parties for giving their support to coalition governments. They have sought to extend measures to compel compliance with Jewish religious law as far as possible. In recent times, their gains have included the imposition of a ban on El Al, the national airline, flying on the sabbath (a prohibition opposed by El Al's management, who argue that it undermines the airline's competitiveness) and the strict prohibition of pig rearing on the 93 per cent of Israel under the ultimate control of the Israel Lands Authority (pork, known as 'white meat', is consumed by many Israeli Jews). A series of disputes over the definition of 'Who is a Jew?' since 1948 have generally ended with concessions being made to Orthodox political and religious leaders.[10] In 1997, a measure which would entrench the Orthodox refusal to accept the validity of non-Orthodox conversions to Judaism as state policy threatened to severely disrupt relations between Israel and the predominantly non-Orthodox Jewish communities in the USA.

The second goal of the religious parties has been narrower: they have tried to win concessions which benefit their own specific constituency of support. In the early days of the state, Ben Gurion wished to encourage a higher Jewish birthrate. The 1953 National Insurance Law gave allowances to families for each child below the age of 18. However, it was realised that this measure disproportionately assisted Arabs, with their larger families, which had not been part of the government's intentions. In 1970, an amendment to the Discharged Soldiers (Return to Work) Law was passed, providing for the payment of extra grants for third and subsequent children of anyone who had performed military service, for however brief a period. This had the effect of excluding most Arabs from these additional payments, since the great majority of them are not called upon to perform military service. Logically, it should have excluded Orthodox Jews studying in yeshivot and not doing military service, but in fact, payments were made to them. When two Arab Knesset members argued that these discretionary payments were discriminatory and that payments should be made to Arabs as well, the Attorney-General found that the payment of statutory payments to people who did not meet the requirements of the law was illegal and should stop, but then the Ministerial Committee on the Interior and Services decided that every full time religious studies student would be entitled to child support. The only existing institutions for full time religious studies were Jewish. There is no doubt that the religious parties lobbied to secure this favourable treatment.[11] Other concessions have amounted to little more than bribes: giving the post of Minister of Religious Affairs to a member of one of the religious parties provides it with a means to channel public money to projects beneficial to its supporters.

At one time, it was said that the religious parties did not care too much about how big Israel was, but they did care about how Jewish it was. This is certainly untrue now. A large majority of the religious public is against giving up any of the West Bank to Palestinian control and opinion polls among Israeli children have shown that religious Jews are the most anti-Arab of all young Israelis. Of the religious parties, only Shas's leadership has taken a less extreme line, stating that it was permissible to give up land in order to save lives.

The secular majority of Israelis detest coercion by the religious minority. Many regard them as parasites who live off the work and donations of others, as people who evade their duty to serve in the army while being content to accept its protection and as killjoys who want to deny the majority the right to enjoy themselves as they please, particularly on the sabbath; their parties are accused of seeking to make Israel a theocracy. These attitudes are not confined to one section of the secular public: supporters of left and right wing secular parties share them. When the far right Tsomet party of Rafael Eitan stood for election in 1992 and took eight seats, it did so on a platform with two main planks: opposition to any territorial concessions to Arabs for the sake of peace and a strong stance against religious 'extortion'. From time to time, there are predictions that, once the conflict with the Arab world is over, there will be a civil war between the religious and the non-religious. 'Civil war' may be too strong a term as, apart from anything else, the great majority of the means of waging war are in the hands of a state machine in which the non-religious have always been dominant and the religious leaders must know that. Nevertheless, some form of decisive clash must occur and it will no doubt come when the religious parties finally exhaust the patience of the secular public. When it does and when the secularists win, it will not only be a victory over religious coercion, but also part of the protracted process of consolidating Israeli nationhood.

An Israeli nation exists. Its creation has been the greatest success of Zionism. Millions of Jews whose ancestors came from many lands and who spoke dozens of languages have become a people with a shared national language and national identity. The differences within this nation are significant, but probably smaller than those between people of diverse origins in the United States, whose nationhood is not seriously questioned. Of the Jewish population of Israel, it is the religious element who have remained most resistant to assimilation into the new nation, with their separate educational institutions, their efforts to insulate themselves as far as possible from the influences of secular Israel and lives regulated by religious observance.

Palestinians in Israel

In 1997, nearly one million Palestinian Arabs were citizens of Israel – almost one in five of its population.[12] They are a fragment of the wider Palestinian people, a national minority living in a state which defines itself as 'the state of the Jewish people', rather than the state of all those – Jews and Arabs – who are its citizens. Most of their land was taken from them during the first 18 years of Israel's existence, when they lived under military government, but the process of dispossession continues. Loss of land turned most into unskilled and semi-skilled workers in the Jewish economy. They faced discrimination, official and unofficial. Many lived in poverty: of the hundred poorest communities in Israel, 99 are Arab. They live with the knowledge that many in Israel consider them a potential 'fifth column' and see their growing numbers as a threat, as recurrent discussion of the 'demographic problem' reveals.[13]

Until the early 1970s, most Palestinians in Israel voted for 'Arab lists' linked to Mapai/Israeli Labour Party. These were headed by people who were able to secure certain gains for themselves, their relatives and supporters by abjectly following their protege's line; often, Mapai made use of *hamula* networks by co-opting an influential member. This changed with the growth of national consciousness after the 1967 war, when the 'Israeli Arabs' came back into contact with other Palestinians in the Israeli-occupied lands and were influenced by the rise of the Palestinian resistance movement in neighbouring lands. After the Israeli government initiated moves to seize additional tracts of Palestinian land in the Galilee, a general strike was called for 30 March 1976. During the clashes which took place on the 'Day of the Land', six Palestinians were shot dead by Israeli police and dozens wounded. This was a turning point for the Palestinians in Israel. In the general election of the following year, about half voted for the electoral list led by Rakah (the Communist Party), known as the Democratic Front for Peace and Equality (DFPE). About a third did not vote at all, many in response to calls by the more radical Abna' al-Balad (Sons of the Village) to boycott the elections.

Rakah was the only non-Zionist party for which Palestinians could vote: attempts to form Arab nationalist groups in the 1950s had been prevented by the authorities. Since 1977, other parties have appeared which sought to appeal to the Arab minority. Rakah saw off the challenge from the Progressive List for Peace (said to have been promoted by the PLO) and from Abna' al-Balad, but in the 1990s faced a more serious challenge from the Islamic movement in Israel, which won control of a number of local councils, including that of Um al-Fahm, and even challenged Rakah/DFPE in its stronghold of Nazareth. The Islamic movement boycotted the 1992 Israeli general election, as it does not accept the legitimacy of the Knesset or any 'Zionist' institution, but in 1996, there was a split: some Islamists allied themselves with the Arab Democratic Party, formed by a defector from the Labour Party, which took four seats in the general election, as against the DFPE's five. One of the latter's seats was taken by Azmi Bishara, representing a more radical grouping called Tajamu'a, which calls for the recognition of the Palestinians in Israel as a national minority.

The State

Following independence in 1948, Ben Gurion acted quickly to ensure the centralisation of authority in the new State of Israel. Of crucial importance was the elimination of military forces outside governmental control, which might embarrass the new state by their actions or even challenge its authority. The Haganah was transformed into Israel's army (officially, the Israeli Defence Forces – IDF) on 30 May 1948, with the Palmach as its elite strike force. A month and a half earlier, Ben Gurion had dissolved the Haganah's National Command (headed by Israel Galili, a member of Mapam), informing it that from then on the Haganah's headquarters would receive orders only from the 'defence director' (Ben Gurion) or his representative. He maintained his overall control following the creation of the state, holding the post of Minister of Defence as well as that of Prime Minister.

The dissolution of LEHI presented no problems. That of the larger Irgun was only completed after the 'Altalena' affair of June 1948. Most of the Irgun's fighters had joined the IDF, but served in units mainly composed of ex-Irgun members; in addition, as Jerusalem was not technically under the authority of the Israeli government in Tel Aviv (according to the terms of the UN partition plan, which Israel treated as operative at that time), independent Irgun and LEHI forces still operated there. A month after Israel declared its independence, the 'Altalena', a ship laden with arms for the Irgun, approached its coast. The government insisted that the arms be handed over to the IDF, and ordered the army to fire on the ship when the Irgun refused. A handful of Irgunists were killed. The dissolution of the Irgun's military apparatus was then completed.[14]

Feelings ran high. Labour Zionists saw the government's action as a measure to head off a possible civil war, but ex-Irgunists smarted with resentment over what they regarded as the imposition of a Mapai monopoly of power by Ben Gurion. Led by the Irgun's former head, Menachem Begin, they established Herut as their political party, which, as the dominant faction in Likud, finally took office in Israel in 1977.

The Palmach played a major role in Israel's victories in 1948, especially against Egypt, but was dominated by Mapam members. Ben Gurion dissolved its command and integrated its units fully into the Israeli army. Mapam supporters were subsequently edged out of the top military positions they had held, and the promotion of those at a more junior level was blocked (as was that of former Irgunists). Ben Gurion had argued for a non-political, professional IDF, but in practice, he equated the national interest with that of his party and his leadership: the IDF's top posts were awarded on the basis of political loyalty, not just ability.

The relationship between political leaders and the military is far more important in Israel than in any Western democratic state.

Military expenditure has always consumed a large percentage of Israel's budget, but such is the public belief in its necessity and so high is the standing of the armed forces that this has never been the target of serious public criticism. There are estimated to be 177,500 personnel serving in the IDF and 427,000 in the reserves, who can be mobilised within hours in an emergency.

Officially, military service is compulsory for all Israeli Jews, although exemption can be claimed on religious grounds. (In 1996, over 6 per cent of draftees refused to serve for religious reasons.) Since 1967, men have served three to three and a half years as conscripts (women are currently liable to 19 months' service), followed by annual rounds of reserve duty amounting to a month or more each time, up to the age of 55.[15] At the height of the Intifada, many reservists were called upon to do two spells of military service within a year. Career officers retire at an earlier age than those in most armies (between 45 and 55 years), which allows younger officers greater promotion opportunities. The pay and 'perks' of career officers have become increasingly generous over the decades, demanding ever more of Israel's military budget – in the recent past, it has been alleged, at the expense of more vital items.[16]

A past military career is a definite asset in most walks of life in Israel. Retired officers have ample opportunities to embark upon a second career. Some lower level officers have gone into 'security' work in Israel or abroad, but most opt for more conventional careers. It is common for former career soldiers to help each other to find work and some use contacts still in the army for the commercial advantage of their new employers.

In political life, men like Moshe Dayan, Ezer Weizman and Yitzhak Rabin have all benefited electorally from their military careers. The absence of a military past is a disadvantage. It counted against Shimon Peres (Rabin's successor as Prime Minister) during his political career, and in the Labour Party vote to determine his successor after his defeat in the 1996 general election, former IDF Chief of Staff, Ehud Barak, won convincingly against the 'yuppie' technocrat, Yossi Beilin.

It is not only its strictly military role and its victories which have given the army its high standing in Israel. It also has the image of a national institution which stands above the sordid squabbles and corrupt practices of political life. Only during the 1980s did signs emerge of an erosion of long established attitudes towards the military. Young Israelis who came from prosperous families and who had good job prospects in civilian life (including kibbutzniks, previously very prominent in the elite units and among the officer corps) felt less inclined than earlier generations to go into military careers, and appeared to regard military service and reserve duty as more of a burden than they had. On the other hand, greater numbers of right-wing religious Zionist Jews were entering precisely those parts of the army where the kibbutzniks had previously been prominent.

The army has played a crucial role in shaping Israelis' identity. It provided the positive image of Jews who stood up and fought those perceived to be threatening them, in contrast to the supposed resignation of Jews in the Diaspora over nearly two thousand years. This is a crucial element in the way Israeli Jews see themselves and are seen by others. The army brought together Israelis of diverse social and political backgrounds as well as very different national origins. They included new immigrants, still poorly integrated into Israeli society and often possessing only a minimal knowledge of Hebrew. The army has been a major integrative force in Israel, reinforcing a sense of shared national destiny among the great majority who served in it, providing them with a crucial reference point in life and helping to induct new citizens into the national collective.

A society in which the army has such a high status is reluctant to see its standing undermined in any way. It is ready to accept censorship on security grounds, even when that is being used to cover up highly questionable practices, such as the use of plain clothes assassination squads against alleged Palestinian activists during the Intifada. The existence of these squads was only officially admitted when a member of one was accidentally killed by a fellow soldier. This caused indignation, which the murder of Palestinians did not.[17] Part of Israeli society (including the press) has become more questioning since the debacle of the 1982 invasion of Lebanon: before that, society as a whole was ready to collude in non-recognition of the truth about military brutality towards national enemies. This included the killing of hundreds of unarmed Palestinian 'infiltrators' in the early 1950s who were either seeking to return home from refugee camps permanently or to recover belongings; the fact that the 1953 Qibya raid, which killed 60 West Bank villagers, was carried out by Israeli soldiers, not enraged civilians responding to an Arab terrorist attack, as the government claimed at the time; the murder of Egyptian prisoners in 1956 at the Mitla Pass and elsewhere; the slaying of Egyptian and Palestine Liberation Army prisoners on the Egyptian front in 1967.[18] Covering up these facts for years allowed the myth of 'the purity of arms' to be maintained, keeping the army's reputation untarnished in the eyes of a public which wanted to believe.

Facing a long term conflict with its neighbours, Israel has developed an advanced weapons industry. It produces aircraft, tanks, guns, missiles, patrol boats and sophisticated systems of weapons guidance and communication. Like other states which began by building weapons industries to supply their own armed forces, Israel has offset development costs and profited by becoming a significant arms exporter, but with even fewer scruples than its competitors: it was apartheid South Africa's main foreign weapons supplier from the mid-1970s[19] and stepped into the breach to sell weapons to the genocidal Guatemalan military regime after the Carter administration cut off US supplies. Arms production is shrouded in secrecy, but '(at) their height, military industries constituted a quarter of Israel's industrial exports and employed a quarter of its industrial labour force'.[20] Workers in these industries are well paid and Jewish: Arab citizens of Israel are not employed for 'security reasons'.

Israel embarked on the development of nuclear weapons in the 1950s and has never signed the Nuclear Non-Proliferation Treaty or admitted to possessing such weapons. In 1986, when Mordechai Vanunu, an ex-employee at the Dimona nuclear plant, supplied the *Sunday Times* with information on Israel's nuclear programme, it was estimated to possess around 100–200 nuclear devices, making it the world's sixth largest nuclear power.[21] All the above factors combine to make Israel a far more militarised society than is commonly realised abroad or even recognised by most Israelis.

Israel's armed forces and their modes of fighting have gradually changed in the 50 years since the state was established.[22] In every war after 1948, air power played a key role. This was very obviously the case in 1967: having gained control of the skies by its surprise attack on the first day of the war, Israel was able to use its air force in support of the campaign on the ground. As most of the land around pre-1967 Israel is open, without tree cover or great mountain chains and deep valleys (apart from Lebanon) to provide ready-made shelter and defensive positions for troops, its sustained domination of the air has given Israel a huge advantage over its Arab rivals.

Following the 1967 war, Israel made increasing use of its air force to strike at the Palestinian guerrilla movement in Jordan (before September 1970) and particularly in Lebanon. Guerrilla positions were hit directly. Raids on alleged guerrilla targets in villages were intended to encourage their inhabitants to turn against the armed Palestinians, blaming them for their sufferings. In border regions, air strikes have been accompanied (or replaced) by shelling. These methods of attack against irregular forces (Palestinian or Lebanese) which are incapable of mounting an equivalent response to either have enabled Israel to minimise its own losses, although how effective they have been against their proclaimed targets is another question: civilians have nearly always taken the brunt of the casualties inflicted.

The Israeli army historically has excelled in certain forms of warfare. It has performed best in wars of movement against Arab conventional forces. In attack, the IDF has orchestrated extremely well the co-ordination between the air force, artillery, tanks, infantry and, on occasion, naval craft. It has skilfully used the 'indirect approach' in attack, by-passing and isolating enemy strongpoints in its initial thrusts, leaving them to be reduced by units following behind those spearheading an advance. The battles with Egypt in 1956 and 1967 are the best examples; this was also the pattern of Israel's attack on the PLO in Lebanon in 1982, until it reached the outskirts of Beirut: it did not let strong-points of resistance such as Beaufort Castle or Ain al-Helweh refugee camp, near Sidon, hold up its main advance. At Beirut and on the Syrian front in 1967, facing fortified positions which could not easily be turned or penetrated, the IDF had less scope to fight in its preferred manner.

Israel's mode of warfare required soldiers who were well trained and disciplined and officered by men who were not only allowed but expected to display initiative and flexibility. Their Arab opponents, by contrast, tended towards rigid adherence to procedure and close supervision by the command structure, a pattern which mirrored other power structures in the Arab world and tended to be reinforced in Egypt and Syria by the influence of Soviet advisers. The 1973 war, in which Egypt and Syria caught Israel off guard with their initial attack, was a gruelling test for the Israeli army. The two Arab states had planned their opening offensives carefully and with imagination (for example, on the Suez Canal, high pressure water hoses were used to breach sand embankments of Israel's Bar Lev line, assumed to be practically impregnable), shocking an Israel whose easy victory in 1967 had left it with an attitude of contempt for Arab fighting abilities. Nevertheless, the IDF rallied well, bringing its strengths into play to hold the Arab advance and then wrest back the initiative.

There are other circumstances in which the IDF has proved less effective. Following its occupation of the whole of southern

Lebanon in 1982, Israel faced popular armed resistance. Ambushes, mines and 'suicide' bombings imposed an escalating toll of dead and wounded upon the Israeli army and depressed the morale of its troops. No collective punishment, raid or assassination diminished the will and capability of the (largely Shi'ite) Lebanese of the south to resist, and in the end, Israel cut its losses and pulled back. Its attempt to hold a 'security zone' on the border with the help of the Israeli-paid and equipped 'South Lebanese Army' (SLA) has simply prolonged the involvement of the IDF in a war of attrition. In the 1990s, the meticulously planned and executed operations of the highly motivated, well trained guerrilla fighters of Hizbullah have proved very effective against the Israeli army. Hizbullah launches surprise attacks on strongpoints held by the SLA/IDF, but has more often struck at Israeli patrols on the move through ambushes and remotely detonated mines. As a result, Israel's overall military posture in Lebanon has become increasingly defensive and reactive: every loss increases pressure from the public and from within the army to leave Lebanon altogether.

The war in southern Lebanon has shown Israel's great sensitivity to military casualties. This goes beyond that of other countries' feelings about losses suffered by their armies. In 1967 and later, commentators claimed that Israelis felt more deeply about the death of their soldiers because the country's population was small and its people were personally affected by each loss; in addition it was claimed that a special Jewish reverence for life also moved them. It may also be that the army's special status in Israel is a factor which works on Israeli sensibilities. Between the beginning of its invasion of Lebanon in June 1982 and its withdrawal to the border zone in 1985, Israel lost about 650 soldiers killed, most during the summer of 1982, prior to the withdrawal of the PLO. Proportionately, this is a fraction of the kind of losses suffered by the opposing sides in the Second World War, but it was enough to make Israel decide to pull back. In a war in which Israelis were genuinely convinced that they were fighting for their existence, or even for vital interests, they would undoubtedly have been prepared to suffer much heavier casualties and still fight on, but they would not do so when they were unconvinced that a useful purpose was being served by staying put.

The army experienced difficulties dealing with the Palestinian Intifada. Its soldiers were not trained to deal with containing protest by hostile civilians. They found the repeated confrontations wearing: soldiers who served in the Gaza Strip, in particular, were generally very glad to depart after a tour of duty there. They were left in no doubt whatsoever that the Palestinians wanted an end to Israeli rule. Senior commanders became concerned about the erosion of the army's morale as it went about what they regarded as 'police duties'. They also worried that training for conventional warfare was being neglected because of the commitment of soldiers to the streets of the West Bank and Gaza Strip in a struggle against people who did not pose a fundamental threat to Israel.

Intelligence

Israel has three major intelligence services: A'man (military intelligence), Mossad (external security service) and Shabak (General Security Service, sometimes called Shin Bet, which is the internal security agency).[23] A secret CIA report seized during the occupation of the US embassy in Tehran in November 1979 and published in Iran provided a detailed account of the structure, tasks and performance of the Israeli intelligence services. Military intelligence was said to employ 7000 personnel, Mossad, 1500–2000 and Shabak, 1000.[24]

A'man focuses on collection and analysis of intelligence on the armed forces of Israel's enemies. Its standing was damaged in 1954 when Egypt arrested a group of its agents who carried out bomb attacks on US institutions in an effort to damage relations between Egypt and the West. A'man suffered a further blow in October 1973, when it failed to predict the Egyptian–Syrian attack, although it had gathered ample information on Egyptian preparations for war. The failure was basically due to the contempt for Arab fighting abilities engendered by Israel's overwhelming victory in 1967. Inter-service rivalry has occurred over the years. Mossad did not hesitate to try to score points at A'man's expense over the 1973 war: Mossad had evaluated the danger of war as high, but Golda Meir's government accepted A'man's assessment.

Mossad was founded in March 1951. Among the world's intelligence services, it is regarded as one of the most effective in gathering information and conducting operations against its country's enemies, including assassinations. The great majority of its agents are recruited and trained in Israel, following service in the army, when their qualities have been subject to the scrutiny of another arm of the state. It has been claimed that Mossad does not recruit Jews in other countries into its service, in order not to jeopardise the security of Jewish communities there, but this is certainly untrue.[25]

Mossad has at its disposal all the paraphernalia of espionage that the most advanced Western security services possess, but in the past, it had one great advantage over them. It was able to recruit people who had spent much of their lives in other countries before migrating to Israel. They were naturally fluent in their first language – sometimes a couple more too – and Jews arrived in such large numbers from so many countries that the pool of potential recruits for service over most of the globe was large. There was no shortage of Arabic speakers, given the hundreds of thousands who had left or been driven out of Arab countries following the creation of the State of Israel. This advantage has tended to wither away over the years, as the proportion of young first generation immigrants in Israel has declined. In particular, there has been comparatively little new migration from the Arab world since the 1960s. The intelligence services are increasingly turning to university trained Arabists.

Mossad has had its setbacks. During its running battle with the Palestinian 'Black September' organisation in 1971–73, agents not only killed a Moroccan waiter they mistook for their Palestinian target in Lillehammer, Norway, but most of the team got caught by the Norwegian police. In 1997, agents in Jordan were captured following an attempt to assassinate a Hamas leader in Amman by spraying a nerve gas into his ear. The victim's bodyguard encountered the agents strolling nonchalantly along a street near the scene of the attack and managed to hold them for long enough to ensure their arrest.

Mossad's worst failure was in Lebanon. It was instrumental in building up close ties for Israel with the Maronite Christian Phalangist party, chiefly on the basis of a shared hostility towards the PLO and the Palestinians. Israel helped to arm and train their militia. When Israel invaded Lebanon in 1982, one of the aims of Defence Minister Ariel Sharon and Mossad was to install a co-operative regime in Beirut. Mossad's leading Lebanese ally, Phalangist leader Bashir Gemayel, was duly elected president of Lebanon by a much depleted parliament under the 'protection' of Phalangist gunmen. He was assassinated (probably at Syria's instigation) a few days later. Israel's Phalangist allies murdered 2000 Palestinian refugees in Sabra and Shatilla refugee camps, after being ushered in by the Israeli army. This brought world condemnation of Israel, as well as the Phalangists. Bashir's brother, Amin Gemayel, was elected president, with the assent of non-Maronite deputies. Induced to sign a peace treaty with Israel, he renounced it in the face of concerted opposition. The divergence of his interests from those of Israel was clear: to be president of Lebanon, he needed the consent of the leaders of non-Maronite communities, which meant that he had to accommodate their political demands up to a certain point. He had to choose between doing Israel's bidding and holding on to the presidency. He opted to work within the Lebanese political system.

Mossad had failed to analyse correctly the role of the Phalangist party in the Lebanese political system and also to evaluate accurately the likely outcome of an Israeli attempt to reshape Lebanon in its interests. It did not anticipate that Israel's alliance with the Phalangists would inflame the hostility of all other Lebanese political factions towards it or that the Phalangists would carry out actions which would bring ignominy upon their allies. Finally, it did not appreciate that the Phalangists viewed their relationship with Israel as a marriage of convenience to serve their own interests in Lebanon: they were not ready to be a second SLA.

In spite of its known fallibility, among many Palestinians there is an over-estimation of Mossad's capabilities (formidable though these certainly are), sometimes expressed in a nonchalant attitude towards security ('Mossad will find out anyway').

Mossad has benefited considerably from its co-operation with Western intelligence services. It established a reputation as a source of dependable information not only on 'Arab terrorism', but on other enemies too: its first great coup, in Western eyes, was to secure a copy of the momentous secret speech denouncing Stalin which Khrushchev delivered to the Communist Party at the Soviet Union's Twentieth Party Congress. On occasion, relations with other services cooled when it trod on their toes: in Britain, in 1988, it emerged that it had run a double agent to gather information on a PLO official suspected of planning violent activities without informing the British security services of the operation. The agent, Ismail Sowan, was arrested and gaoled, and a five-man Mossad cell based at the London embassy was ordered out by an irate Margaret Thatcher.

In June 1996, Danny Yatom (the first serving head whose name could be published in Israel) took charge of a troubled Mossad. There was reported to be internal strife in Mossad; it was less certain of its role following the end of the Cold War and the signing of the DoP with the PLO and a peace treaty with Jordan; there have been suggestions that the calibre of Mossad agents is declining:

> 'Among many of the people who would have gone into Mossad, there is a feeling that there is peace, so it is no longer necessary to do what their fathers did. There has been a drop in the charm

of the security forces,' a former Mossad official, now working in a political think-tank, complained.

Today's princes and princesses are more likely to move abroad in search of higher pay or join one of the new, highly-successful hi-tech firms flourishing in the country's coastal cities, where the threat of war seems distant ... Peace and MTV are sapping Mossad's strength.[26]

The third key security service is the Shabak. It keeps an eye on Israeli Jews whose views and activities place them outside the national consensus: leftists such as the Jews who take/took part in the Communist Party, 'Derech HaNitzotz' group and the Alternative Information Centre,[27] anti-nuclear activists and the extreme right groups inspired by Meir Kahane. Jewish society has always treated the left as a greater threat than the right, which was an underlying factor in its failure to prevent the assassination of Prime Minister Rabin in 1995.

Shabak watched the remaining Arab communities in Israel after 1948 and then, following the 1967 war, extended its operations to the West Bank and Gaza Strip. Jordanian police files on Palestinian activists, captured intact in Jerusalem and Hawara, proved invaluable in countering the first attempts to organise a West Bank-based guerrilla struggle. From the outset, Shabak sought to recruit collaborators among the Palestinians by intimidation, blackmail and bribery. It became widely understood that those who were prepared to work with the Shabak would find life easier: a formerly hard to obtain permit to build a house would be granted, goods 'delayed in customs' would be released or a family member in exile would be allowed a visit. (It could be very devious too, giving apparent signs of favour to militant activists to foster the suspicion among their comrades that they were informers. Even talking to them in an apparently friendly way in the street or shaking hands with them upon leaving their homes following an unsolicited visit could do the trick.)

Most Shabak agents operating against the Palestinians needed to have a good command of Arabic. This has been used not only to eavesdrop on conversations, tap phonecalls and read letters, leaflets and other printed material, but also during interrogation of detained Palestinians. The great majority of convictions of Palestinians arrested during the occupation were obtained by Shabak through the use of torture.

Israel is unique in having effectively legalised torture. Other states, including most in the region, practise it in more brutal forms, but deny doing so, not caring to offer legal excuses. Since 1967, there have been repeated claims by Palestinians that they had been tortured after being arrested. These were routinely denied by Israel. However, Shabak made the mistake of acting against serving Israeli soldiers as it acts against Arabs – not so much by torturing them, as by lying to the courts. In 1982, it induced Izzat Nafsu, a Circassian officer serving in Lebanon, to confess to treasonous actions which he did not commit. He received an 18-year prison sentence. It was admitted during Nafsu's successful appeal in 1987 that torture and perjury were routine in Shabak.[28] In 1984, it attempted to frame Brigadier-General Yitzhak Mordechai with killing two Palestinian prisoners involved in a bus hijacking, when in fact, the deed had been done by Shabak agents at the order of Shabak's head, Avraham Shalom.[29] These incidents, not the thousands of pages of Arab testimony about torture, prompted the appointment of an investigative commission under former Supreme Court President, Judge Moshe Landau. In October 1987, the Landau Commission found that, for 16 years, Shabak personnel had routinely lied to the courts about the methods used to obtain confessions. It drew a curious conclusion from its findings. To spare the interrogators having to practise deception concerning their methods, it declared that the 'exertion of a moderate amount of physical pressure' to secure confessions was justified and, in a secret annex to its report, laid down exact guidelines about what could and could not be done to a prisoner. What had mainly concerned Landau was telling lies, not brutality towards prisoners.[30]

Organisations such as Amnesty International have called for the secret guidelines to be published: if they do not sanction practices which contravene international law, that should not be a problem. The evidence is that they do. Since the Landau Commission's recommendations were approved by the government, prisoners have reported being beaten, tied in painful positions for extended periods of time (backwards over the seat of a chair, for example, with hands and feet tied together beneath it), hung from ceiling level pipes by their wrists and being shaken violently. The story of the circumstances in which the Landau Commission was established, its findings and the status accorded its recommendations in Israel reveals much about the workings of the Shabak, but is also indicative of the ethical corruption of the Israeli legal system.

As far as Jewish citizens of Israel are concerned, it works to high standards. But this is the legal system of an entity which defines itself as the 'State of the Jewish People', not the state of its citizens. Israel's courts uphold the laws passed by its government in accordance with this principle. Israel has passed laws and manipulated legal provisions which it inherited from previous rulers of Palestine in order to exercise control over the Palestinians under its rule and to seize Palestinian land. This is one of the reasons why Israel does not have a constitution. In other states, similar documents set out the basic rights of citizens, and unjust laws may be challenged by reference to rights enshrined in a constitution. If Israel had adopted a Western-style constitution, this might have provided recourse to its Arab citizens against the policies of the state towards them. (The other major problem was that it would involve tackling the issue of the status of the Jewish religion and Halacha – Jewish religious law – in Israel.)

The great majority of the territory which became part of Israel in 1948 was not under Jewish ownership at the time. Seventy years of land purchasing efforts had brought only 6.6 per cent of Palestine into Jewish ownership. Now there was an opportunity to take the land at little or no cost, and it was seized with both hands. Measures were devised to allow the transfer of most of it to Jewish control – primarily, to the Israel Lands Authority. The property of the Palestinians who had been expelled from the land was seized under the terms of the Absentees' Property Law of 1950. This did not satisfy the state's appetite. It took most of the land of the Palestinians who had remained within its borders and had become Israeli citizens. All those who had moved to territory controlled by hostile forces between 29 November 1947 and 1 September 1948 were classified as 'absentees', including people who found themselves at the end of the 1948 war under Israeli rule. The 'present absentees'' property was treated in the same way as that of people who actually were outside Israel.[31]

A very clear example of the perversion of justice in Israel was the use to which the authorities put a measure which was ostensibly intended to promote agricultural production. An area would be declared 'closed' under Article 125 of the Defence (Emergency) Regulations of 1945, introduced by Britain. For 'security reasons', Palestinian farmers would be denied permits to gain access to their fields in the closed area. As a result, the Minister of Agriculture could soon declare the land to be 'uncultivated'. He then used his powers under the Emergency Regulations (Cultivation of Waste Lands) Ordinance, 5709-1949 to 'ensure that it is cultivated' by handing it over to someone else to farm. The 'someone else' was invariably a Jewish settler.[32]

Israeli laws confer rights upon Jews which are denied to non-Jews. They permit the kind of discriminatory practices which, if applied to the disadvantage of Jews in other countries, would certainly invite charges of anti-semitism. Thus, 93 per cent of Israel's territory is controlled by the official Israel Lands Authority, which enforces the Jewish National Fund's prohibitions against non-Jews being sold, leased or allowed to live on the land. This is manifestly unjust to Palestinian citizens of the state (to say nothing about those excluded from it): they need more land, and part of the ILA's land was taken from them in the first place, but they are unable even to purchase back what was their own property.

In August 1986, when Israel had a Labour–Likud coalition government, the Knesset passed an 'Anti-Racist Law'. An anti-racism bill had been introduced to curb the activity of Meir Kahane's Kach party, whose demands for the 'transfer' of all Arabs out of the 'Land of Israel' had been the subject of fierce criticism in Israel and abroad. The bill was limited to the criminalisation of public statements 'inciting to racism or with the intent to provoke racism': it would not prohibit discriminatory practices, and so, for example, posed no threat to the Jewish exclusivist policy of the ILA/JNF. The religious parties objected that the proposed law would threaten Halacha (Jewish religious law), which demands certain discriminatory measures against non-Jews. After some delay, the Labour Party, anxious to conciliate potential coalition partners, exempted from the law material which 'aims at preserving the character, uniqueness or worship of a religion, provided this was not done with the object of inciting to racism'. When the final vote on the bill was taken, a smiling Kahane raised both hands in favour: he maintained that all the discriminatory measures he advocated were based upon religious principles. For 'balance', another law went through the Knesset in parallel: it prohibited Israelis from having contacts with activists or representatives of 'terrorist organisations', effectively making illegal meetings with the PLO and its officials, whatever their purpose.[33]

Israeli citizens who are dissatisfied with the decisions of a lower level court may seek to pursue their appeal at the Supreme Court in Jerusalem. This option was also available, in many instances, to the Palestinians living under Israeli occupation after 1967. The success rate for appeals by Jews is very low: that for Palestinians is negligible. In 1987, Dr Avishai Ehrlich of Tel Aviv University made a study of all the appeals presented to the Supreme Court in the second half of 1986 – apparently the first time anyone had made such an analysis. He found that in only 6 per cent of cases was the appeal successful. Not one of the 59 appeals presented by Palestinians from the West Bank and Gaza Strip succeeded. Palestinians have drawn their own conclusions from their lack of success with the Supreme Court. Ehrlich's study showed that, although Palestinians made up 17 per cent of Israel's population, they presented only 12 per cent of Supreme Court appeals; Palestinians in the 1967 occupied territories made up a quarter of the people under Israel's rule, but only presented 13 per cent of appeals.[34]

The Supreme Court in Jerusalem has been influenced in its decisions by the outlook of its judges, who, like their counterparts elsewhere, are nearly always pillars of the establishment. When it has come to dealing with Palestinians, it has reflected the views of an establishment which not only upholds certain class values, but also Zionist values. It has almost invariably been prepared to accept government justifications of questionable practices towards Arabs by appeals to 'reasons of security'. This allowed Shabak and the army in the West Bank and Gaza Strip to act with little legal restraint. The laws and Military Orders which operate in the areas occupied in 1967 were carefully framed so that the army, Shabak and the Israeli government have a free hand to do virtually as they please.

Israel prides itself on being a state where the rule of law prevails, but 'law' and 'justice' are different concepts, as Israel's treatment of all the Palestinians under its rule has shown. The central position of one form of law in Jewish religious observance and the firm belief of most Jews around the world in the importance of the rule of law has made Israel a state which attaches great weight to correct legal forms, even when they allow actions which are manifestly unjust. This has enabled most of its citizens and supporters to convince themselves of the justice of practically each and every measure taken by Israel which has an adverse impact upon the Palestinians it rules. It is a factor in Israel's strength because it allows good hearted people to avoid facing the contradiction between two cherished beliefs: in Zionism and the State of Israel, and in justice.

At the birth of political Zionism, Herzl and most of those who worked with him looked towards a day when, as they saw it, Jews would be a people like other peoples. Zionism has created an Israeli Jewish nation, but its democratic life has been devalued by the imperatives of the Zionist mission; the rule of law has been degraded by the abuse of justice by Israel in its dealings with the Palestinians; the state has won its wars, but Israel remains on guard against all its neighbours, heavily militarised and its political life distorted by the continuing conflict with the Palestinian people. 'Normalisation' will not be achieved until Israel resolves its conflict with the Palestinian people on the basis of equality and the acknowledgement that they are entitled to the rights of a people like other peoples.

3

Renewal and Retreat

There were many people on the move around the world in the second half of the 1940s. Tens of millions were displaced by war and border changes in Europe and East Asia. Millions more in the Indian subcontinent fled from or to the new states created by another partition plan. Compared to them, the number of Palestinian refugees – about 700,000 – seems small. To know this statistic and to be aware of the wretched conditions in which these people now found themselves struggling to survive is yet to lack a full appreciation of what happened to them and to the Palestinian people as a whole.

When Poles were made to leave the eastern regions of pre-war Poland which were incorporated into the Soviet Union in 1945, the historic core territories of their country remained largely intact (although devastated by war). A Polish state (albeit under a regime detested by most of its citizens) existed. Although millions of Germans were driven from their homes east of the Oder river, the bulk of historic Germany remained German and the means existed to rebuild a German state (or two, as it turned out ...). For all the suffering that it entailed, the flight of Hindus and Muslims from their old homes to India and Pakistan respectively did not fundamentally undermine these entities as states or societies.

What happened to the Palestinians was of another order. A majority of the Arab population were obliged to leave their homes and 78 per cent of their country passed to the control of another people. There had not been a Palestinian Arab state before and there was not one at the end of the 1948 conflict. A society shaken by the events of the previous 30 years was shattered by what occurred in that war. No unifying national institution survived. Before the war, Palestinian Arabs had lived in a single territory, under one administration; at its end, they were dispersed under five different sovereignties.

National extinction seemed to await them. They might survive as individuals, but as a people with their own identity and national rights, they faced disappearance without their nationhood ever having been allowed expression in an independent state. This was what Israel's leaders wished to happen. They had never acknowledged the Palestinian Arabs as a people with national rights over their homeland: now that they had been comprehensively defeated, they were expected to accept the State of Israel as a fait accompli and not only to surrender what they had once possessed, but also any claim to an identity which linked them to this land. With extraordinary determination and endurance, the Palestinians denied Israel that final victory, rising up from the wreckage of 'The Catastrophe' to affirm that a Palestinian people exists and will not be denied its rights as a nation.

The Exiles

In the course of the 1948 war, expelled Palestinians normally fled to the nearest accessible Arab-controlled territory. Sometimes, the subsequent advance of the Israeli army meant that they had to move a second or third time. Those forced out of the Galilee region mainly went to Lebanon or Syria; Palestinians in the central part of the country generally fled to what became known as the West Bank, apart from those who lived in Jaffa: surrounded by Jewish-inhabited territory and Zionist military forces, most fled by sea, ending up in Lebanon. In the south-west, Palestinians crowded into the shrunken region under Egyptian control which became known as the Gaza Strip. A few, richer or with helpful personal contacts, travelled further afield.

Conditions for all but the most fortunate were very hard. Local residents often tried hard to help the displaced at first, but their own resources soon gave out. Charitable societies and a few foreign-based agencies gave what assistance they could. In 1950, the United Nations Relief and Works Agency for Palestinian Refugees (UNRWA) began operations. Palestinian attitudes towards it have been ambivalent. It provided registered refugees with food rations and basic health care. Its educational services helped to supply refugee children with the means to earn a living and sometimes to reach university. It was a provider of employment itself. Its support by UN member states has been seen as an acknowledgement by the 'international community' of its responsibilities to the Palestinian people.

At the same time, it has also been regarded as an agency used to keep Palestinian discontent under control, its drip-feed assistance serving to keep in check the disruptive potential of hundreds of thousands of desperate people who were resentful of the ineffectualness of Arab governments in securing the restitution of their rights and unreconciled to the loss of their lands and homes. In this connection, some have seen it as significant that the largest donor state to UNRWA by far has been the United States, principal arms supplier and financier of Israel.

The great majority of the Palestinian refugees (a majority even more pronounced in the camps) were of peasant origin. They had lost all that they possessed and their working skills were not in short supply in their places of refuge. They retained an unwavering conviction that it was their right to return to lands which they had not relinquished voluntarily. It was a conviction which they passed on to their children. In the collective memory, life before Zionism became idealised, its more negative aspects increasingly overlooked with each passing year. The past seemed all the more beautiful in contrast to the wretched present. To this day, children born in the camps give the name of the village where their grandparents or great-grandparents lived when asked where they come from, rather than, say, Ain al-Hilweh or Beach Camp. They frequently grow up among people of the same origin: in 1948, villagers forced to leave their homes usually moved as a group and stayed together in the camps. Many families still possess the keys to houses they left in Palestine, most of which no longer exist.[1]

It was refugees who, from 1968 onwards, formed the mainstay of the resurgent Palestinian national movement. In the 1960s, dogmatic foreign Marxists were critical of that movement for its reliance on their support. This, they said, was no substitute for the support of the 'Arab working class': the refugees came from a petit bourgeois class background and could not pose a consistent challenge to Zionism or imperialism because of their class character. The reality was that there was not a mighty Arab working class, seething with revolutionary fervour and only awaiting a call to action. The Palestinian resistance movement could only count on its own people and the refugees proved determined and courageous. Yasser Arafat once proclaimed, 'We have nothing to lose but our tents'[2] and, if this was an exaggeration, it did reflect how the refugees felt. Unlike Marx's proletarians, they had not been drawn en masse into large scale industrial production, but like them, they were propertyless, they had a strong potential for collective organisation (if in their places of residence rather than of work) and they were without any vested interest in the established order. A revolutionary role was forced upon them by circumstances, as any determined effort to take on Israel would lead to confrontations with those who endorsed or feared to challenge the new regional status quo.

Israel has frequently claimed that the Arab states deliberately kept the 'refugee problem' alive by confining the refugees in camps instead of allowing them to resettle. It said that they wished to use the refugees as a tool against Israel, hostility towards which was the only thing upon which they could unite. The truth was rather different. Palestinians who could earn a steady income often left the camps. The biggest obstacles to doing so existed in Lebanon, for internal reasons: the authorities did not want a population which was overwhelmingly Sunni Muslim by religion to settle and upset its fragile Maronite Christian-dominated sectarian political system. Palestinian refugees themselves opposed any scheme to change their status which would bring into question their right to return to Palestine. When, shortly after coming to power, Nasser's government planned to transfer some of the refugees out of the Gaza Strip to the north Sinai coast, there were widespread protests in the camps: people did not want to be moved further away from their homes.[3]

At first, the expelled Palestinians believed that their exile would be brief. They looked to those with far more power than them to secure their rights. On 11 December 1948, the United Nations General Assembly passed Resolution 194, which included the statement that:

> the refugees wishing to return to their homes and live at peace with their neighbours should be permitted to do so at the earliest practicable date, and that compensation should be paid for the property of those choosing not to return and for the loss of or damage to property.

The UN has reaffirmed that resolution annually, but it has never been backed by measures to ensure Israeli compliance. Neither did it seem that the Arab regimes defeated in the 1948 war would do anything effective in their support. Young Palestinian intellectuals from among the expelled tired of waiting and resolved to act.[4]

Some saw their best hope for the future lying in political change in the wider Arab world. The communist parties, which called for radical political and social change, attracted few. Their ideology was objectionable to many in a society in which the influence of religion was strong and they had, in any case, condemned themselves irreparably in the eyes of the great majority by their support for the partition resolution in 1947. Ba'athism, which claimed to combine pan-Arabism with socialism, won a few adherents. Palestinians were instrumental in founding the Arab Nationalists' Movement (ANM). Its leading figure was George Habash, a doctor by profession, whose family were Christians from Lydda, expelled when that city fell to Israeli forces in 1948. Habash and other Palestinians in the ANM saw Arab unity as the key to winning the liberation of Palestine. They considered that the failure of the Arab armies against Israel in 1948 was mainly due to the nature of the Arab regimes, which they saw as corrupt, pro-imperialist entities which were solely concerned with looking after their own selfish interests and those of their foreign masters. They believed that Nasser had shown the way forward when he took control of the Suez Canal, confronted Britain and France, carried out internal social and economic reforms and, particularly, when he sought to encourage Arab unity: a united Arab world under a popular nationalist government could surely mobilise the resources to defeat Israel. After the 1967 war, the Palestinian ANM members joined with two other groups to establish the Popular Front for the Liberation of Palestine (PFLP).

Others took a very different view. They gravitated towards the group which emerged at the end of the 1950s as al-Fatah, a name derived from the (reversed) Arabic acronym of the Palestinian National Liberation Movement. Yasser Arafat emerged as first among equals in Fatah's leadership. (Subsequently, he was always prepared to take more account of the views of his fellow Fatah veterans than of other Palestinian leaders, including later recruits to Fatah itself.) The political convictions of these individuals varied somewhat. Salah Khalaf, known as Abu Iyad, held leftist views, while Khalid al-Hassan was conservative in outlook; Arafat himself had fought with the Muslim Brotherhood in 1948. However, they and others such as Khalil al Wazir (Abu Jihad) and Faruq Qaddoumi (Abu Lutf) united around certain central beliefs which became those of Fatah.

Fatah believed in the desirability of Arab unity, but thought that it was more likely to be realised through the struggle to liberate Palestine than as a precondition for undertaking that struggle. It also believed that differences over questions such as whether Palestine should develop on socialist lines should not be allowed to take precedence over the need to unite around the central objective of the liberation of Palestine. This 'Palestine first' approach allowed Fatah to embrace a wide range of views within its ranks, from leftists who believed in a clearly defined two-stage advance to socialism, via national liberation, to bourgeois Palestinians who contributed generously to its finances and were none too keen on any notion of class warfare. Fatah believed that the Palestinians had to win back control of their own destiny and this could only be done if they organised themselves for the liberation of their homeland, rather than relying on others to restore their rights to them.

Fatah argued that armed struggle was the only way to liberate Palestine. It did not expect that the Palestinians would defeat Israel on their own, but believed that they could do so with strong Arab allies and international support. Fatah believed that, before long, Israel would go to war against the neighbouring Arab states and defeat them. The discredited regimes would fall, to be replaced by popular nationalist governments ready to make a wholehearted commitment to support the Palestinian struggle. However, Fatah considered that the Palestinians should not allow themselves to be drawn into the internal politics of the Arab countries: this would only divert their energies from their central mission. Fatah's views on armed struggle changed over the following decades, but its commitment to Palestinian independent decision making and to non-interference in the affairs of Arab states remained steady, even if events forced it off course at times.

Fatah's early membership came together partly through the magazine *Filastinuna* (Our Palestine), published in Beirut. Sources disagree on the exact date of its foundation, but it clearly occurred in the late 1950s. Preparations for the launching of the armed struggle soon began. Money was collected from members and supporters for the purchase of arms. Contacts were made with potential sources of advice, training and material assistance, including the government of Algeria (brought to power after a gruelling eight-year war of liberation in July 1962) and supporters within the Syrian armed forces.

The armed struggle was launched on the night of 31 December 1964–1 January 1965. The operation, directed against an Israeli scheme to divert water from the Jordan, was announced in a communique issued in the name of 'Al Assifah' (The Storm). Fatah preferred not to admit responsibility for its first attacks until it was confident that the armed struggle had been successfully launched, but, once it did, it still used the name 'Al Assifah' in communiques to refer to its armed forces.

In June 1967, the fateful clash which Fatah had foreseen took place. After a period of rising tension, Israel launched a devastating surprise attack on Egypt, Jordan and Syria. It destroyed most of their air forces on the ground, thereby securing total mastery of the air within hours of the conflict beginning. Within six days, Israel crushed the armies of its Arab opponents and conquered the West Bank and Gaza Strip, as well as Egypt's Sinai Peninsula and Syria's Golan Heights. This debacle plunged the Arab world into gloom. It could not be viewed in the same light as the defeat of the Arab armies in 1948 under the corrupt old regimes. Particularly shocking was the fact that Egypt, under the nationalist leadership of President Nasser and deeply popular throughout the Arab world, had been defeated so quickly and decisively.

Fatah decided to relaunch the armed struggle as quickly as possible following the 1967 war. Its hope was to escalate the conflict in the newly-occupied Palestinian territories until it developed into a popular uprising. Organisers, including Arafat, infiltrated into the West Bank with relative ease, re-establishing links with Fatah activists and winning new recruits. Armed operations re-commenced in August 1967, but did not unfold as hoped. Israeli counter-measures were extremely effective and the great majority of West Bank Palestinians felt they had too much to lose by engaging in a violent conflict with Israel. Fatah's guerrilla networks were smashed and Arafat himself barely escaped back to Jordan. The armed struggle (save in the Gaza Strip over the next three years, where the PFLP managed to conduct a more sustained guerrilla campaign) now became one mainly fought on the borders of Israeli-controlled territory. The relative weakness of the government of Jordan following the 1967 war allowed Palestinian guerrillas the opportunity to establish bases there, from which they mounted hit and run attacks across the river Jordan. Israel responded by shelling and bombing alleged 'terrorist bases'. On 21 March 1968, it made a large scale ground assault upon guerrillas in the Jordan valley town of Karameh.

In his writings on 'people's war', Mao Zedong had advised that, in the face of an attack by superior enemy forces, the revolutionary fighters should retreat and give battle when conditions favoured them, rather than risking heavy losses to their own forces.[5] Fatah's leadership knew that an Israeli attack was coming and it was familiar with Mao's advice, but decided that its guerrillas should stay in Karameh and fight. This was an example of the tactical shrewdness it has often displayed. It believed that the advantages to be gained by demonstrating that its forces were ready to confront the Israelis would outweigh the anticipated loss in casualties. So it proved. Palestinian losses were heavy, but the

Israeli attackers retreated with about 25 dead and their mission of liquidating the guerrillas unaccomplished. They left behind tanks disabled by Jordanian artillery fire, which were towed in triumph through Amman. Fatah celebrated the outcome as a victory, and so it was seen throughout the Arab world.

Thousands of volunteers, including non-Palestinians, hurried to join the fidai'in ('men who sacrifice themselves' – the Arabic term commonly used for the fighters). The majority joined Fatah, but others turned to rival organisations such as the PFLP. The relationship between the Palestinian national movement and the Arab states was transformed. Such was the popularity of the Palestinian resistance that it was politically advantageous to take a strong public stance in its support. Some Arab states created fidai'in organisations which were aligned with them, notably Saiqa (backed by Syria) and the Arab Liberation Front (backed by the Iraqi Ba'athist regime).

The growth of Palestinian political activism had impelled the Arab states to support the establishment of the Palestine Liberation Organisation in 1964. Ahmad Shuqairy, who had previously served as a diplomat, became Chairman of the PLO Executive Committee, the organisation's highest post. National institutions were set up from above, including the General Union of Palestinian Workers (now Palestine Trade Union Federation), General Union of Palestinian Women and the Palestine Liberation Army, a conventional military force whose units were placed under the control of the Arab states in which they were based.

This was essentially a means for keeping Palestinian nationalist activity within strictly defined bounds, acceptable to most Arab states. As such, it was treated with some scorn by Fatah, but that attitude changed in the post-Karameh conditions. With popular support and the backing of a previously suspicious Nasser, Fatah was able to secure a majority in the Palestine National Council (PNC – the body responsible for determining the policy of the PLO and electing its leadership) and PLO Executive Committee in 1969. It might have chosen to allow the PLO to wither away and stressed its own leading role at this point, but chose to take over and work through the established machinery. The PLO had a representative role acknowledged by the Arab states, and it seemed advantageous to build upon that. In addition, the PLO offered a framework within which Fatah could work with other Palestinian organisations rather than attempt to create a new one with them.

The consequences of this decision were overwhelmingly positive. The PLO won increasing international recognition as the representative of the Palestinians, highlighted by the invitation extended by the United Nations in 1974 to Yasser Arafat, as Chairman of the PLO Executive Committee, to address the General Assembly. One drawback has been that Fatah and the PLO have become too closely identified. The world tended to see Fatah's best-known leaders in their PLO roles and had little sense of Fatah existing as a distinct political organisation. Many of the most capable Fatah members were absorbed into the PLO machinery, and were therefore able to give less attention to the political and organisational strengthening of their movement. Short term gains might be made by the recruitment of people through the powers of patronage which control of the PLO opened up to Fatah, but that kind of support is liable to dilute an organisation's political strength and to fall away in a serious crisis. Over the following decades, Fatah went through a process of 'hollowing out': its organisational structure continued to exist and it remained the dominant political force among Palestinians, but its politically committed core of members became weaker.

One problem which has never been resolved in the PLO is that of democracy. The great majority of delegates to the PNC, which decides the PLO's policy and elects its leadership, were either chosen by their organisations or appointed as 'independents'. After 1969, Fatah always commanded a majority through the votes of its own delegates and Fatah-aligned independents. The PFLP and DFLP periodically criticised this arrangement and called for 'democratisation' of the PLO. They never persisted in campaigning on the issue, as they normally gained a larger representation in the PNC under the existing system than they would if a more democratic selection process were to be put in place.

Within a very short space of time, the Palestinian resistance movement achieved a great deal. It reasserted the existence of the Palestinian Arabs as a people with their own identity and a cause which they believed to be just. It restored a sense of dignity and pride to them. The tenacity with which, during the trials of the following years, the Palestinians – especially those in the camps – maintained their support for the PLO is a tribute to what the movement headed by Fatah accomplished after the 1967 war. Palestinian support for the resistance movement was cross-class and multi-generational. In Jordan and Lebanon, the two states in which it had secured the greatest freedom of action by the end of 1969, it took effective control of the refugee camps. Residents participated in various popular committees and benefited from the services established by the PLO and its affiliates, which reached their fullest development in Lebanon in the 1970s, when they included the medical services of the Palestine Red Crescent Society and the co-operative workshops of Samed.[6]

Their damaging factional strife and the defeat of 1948 had discredited the traditional elites in Palestinian society. From the exiled communities had emerged a new bourgeoisie, scattered across the Arab world and beyond, but with a large concentration in the oil-rich Gulf states. From the late 1960s, the great majority gave their support to the PLO, under Fatah leadership. The leftists of the PFLP and the breakaway Democratic Popular Front for the Liberation of Palestine (DPFLP, soon to drop 'Popular' from its name) were more successful in winning support among sectors of the Palestinian intelligentsia, such as students and teachers.

The level of support for the PLO inside historic Palestine at first lagged behind that outside, in part because of Israeli repression against activists of PLO member organisations but also because of the residual influence of pro-Jordanian notables from the traditionally powerful families. The mayors of the West Bank's towns belonged to this group. Israel left them in office (apart from Rouhi al-Khatib, mayor of Jerusalem, dismissed immediately after Israel annexed the eastern part of the city), anticipating that, in the near future, it might conclude an agreement with Jordan which would restore some form of Jordanian rule over most of the West Bank.[7] The PLO called for a boycott of the mayoral elections in 1972, but in 1976, pro-PLO candidates stood and swept away most of the old guard, strikingly demonstrating the political ascendancy achieved by the PLO on the West Bank. 'The only democracy in the Middle East', unhappy with the result, was careful not to give West Bank Palestinians another chance to vote for their leaders prior to the signing of the DoP.

Aims and Means

There have often been fierce debates among Palestinian political groups about the aims of the Palestinian national movement and how to attain them. These took place in far from ideal conditions, the Palestinians being dispersed geographically, subjected to pressures from Arab host governments and engaged in a conflict which waxed and waned, but never ceased. Policy decisions of the PLO and its constituent organisations were influenced by Palestinian public opinion, inter-Palestinian politics, the regional balance of power and the demands of international diplomacy.

In the heady days before Black September in 1970, when Jordan clamped down on the fidai'in, the options of the Palestinian resistance seemed wide open. The nationalist organisations tackled questions of enduring importance to the liberation movement: How should the Palestinian resistance define its ultimate aim? Who were its friends and potential allies and who were its enemies? What strategy should be followed to change the balance of power in the Palestinians' favour and, in particular, how great a part should armed struggle play in it?

Movements of national liberation have often changed their tactics and adopted new means of seeking their goals, but what normally remains constant are those goals themselves. This was certainly true of successful organisations such as the ANC in South Africa, ZANU in Zimbabwe and the Eritrean People's Liberation Front (EPLF). The PLO has differed in altering its aims as well as its strategy and tactics: indeed, changing its aims has formed part of its strategy. The overall trend was one of retreat from the aim of the liberation of Palestine to that of establishing a state in a fraction of the country.

When the PLO was originally established, it adopted a Palestine National Charter, which set forth its aims and beliefs. The Charter repeatedly referred to the liberation of Palestine, but Article 24 stipulated, 'This Organisation shall not exercise any territorial sovereignty over the West Bank (region) of the Hashemite Kingdom of Jordan, the Gaza Strip or the Himmah area.'[8] These were those parts of Palestine which were then under the control of Arab states. This qualification was chiefly required to assure Jordan that its sovereignty over the West Bank was not under challenge from the PLO. However, according to Article 2, 'Palestine, within the boundaries it had during the period of the British Mandate, is an indivisible territorial unit.' This at least implied that the Palestinians should eventually be able to decide their future as one people in the whole of Palestine. Article 7 stated that 'Jews of Palestinian origin shall be considered Palestinian if they desire to undertake to live in loyalty and peace in Palestine', but Article 6 had defined Palestinians as 'those Arab citizens who, until 1947, had normally resided in Palestine' and their descendants, thus excluding all but a small proportion of the Jews of Israel. Clearly, they were not to be allowed to stay in Palestine.

The Palestine National Charter was radically amended in July 1968, when the resistance forces were beginning to flex their muscles.[9] They showed their independence and commitment to Palestinian control over all Palestine by deleting the existing

Article 24 (see above). The old Article 7 was replaced by a new Article 6, which declared, 'The Jews who had normally resided in Palestine until the beginning of the Zionist invasion will be considered Palestinians.' This formulation was vaguer than the one it replaced. As this could be identified as having occurred as far back as the 1880s, this was a narrower definition than that of the 1964 Charter. The other major change to the Charter was that it stated very clearly how the Palestinians were to realise their aims. Article 9 declared, 'Armed struggle is the only way to liberate Palestine. Thus it is the overall strategy, not merely a tactical phase.'

The Charter was not officially amended again until 1996, but, in reality, the PLO's aims and its strategy changed radically after 1968. When Arafat outraged the PFLP and others in 1989 by declaring the Charter *'caduc'* (no longer operative) during a visit to France, he was simply telling the truth. The changes began within months of the Charter having been amended. In 1969, under Fatah's leadership, the PNC declared the aim of the Palestinians to be 'a Palestinian democratic state ... free of all forms of religious and social discrimination'.[10] PLO spokespeople explained that this would be a state in which Jews, Muslims and Christians would be equal.[11] This was not without its problems as a goal on the theoretical as well as practical level. It defined the entire population of the future Palestinian state in religious terms, when, for most Israelis, being Jewish was a matter of *national* identity; Palestinian organisations (with the partial exception of the DPFLP) were not prepared to accept that.

The adoption of this aim was a very significant change in the Palestinian position towards Israeli Jews. It meant that their presence in Palestine was now accepted as a fact of life, even if the way in which it had come about was not regarded as legitimate. If the PLO realised its goal, they would lose a Jewish state, but be accorded equal personal rights in a unitary Palestinian state. As the PLO insisted upon the right of the Palestinian refugees to return home, they would, in principle, be expected to give back the land Israel had expropriated after the 1948 war. Nevertheless, after all the Palestinians had suffered and lost, adopting this aim was a magnanimous gesture. The PLO had accepted the principle of the land being shared by Palestinian Arabs and those who were then Israeli Jews within the framework of one state.

This aim might have been elaborated to become more inclusive and offer a clearer vision of a just and democratic country. Instead, step by step, the PLO embraced national separation, coming to advocate a Palestinian state in the West Bank and Gaza Strip alongside the State of Israel. In 1974, when, in the wake of the war of the previous October, it appeared that there might be Arab–Israeli talks resulting in Israel withdrawing from occupied Arab lands, the PLO staked its claim to any Palestinian territory relinquished. The 12th PNC approved a ten-point programme, the second point of which stated:

> The Liberation Organisation will employ all means, and first and foremost armed struggle, to liberate Palestinian territory and to establish the independent combatant national authority for the people over every part of Palestinian territory that is liberated.[12]

Although presented as a transitional step towards a democratic state in the whole of Palestine, this was only a temporary concession by the advocates of a 'two-state solution' to those still strongly adhering to the aim adopted in 1969. The decisive step towards declaring the PLO's goal to be the 'two-state solution' had been taken. Finally, the 18th PNC, which took place in November 1988, towards the end of the first year of the Intifada, issued a Palestinian Declaration of Independence. It stated that UN General Assembly Resolution 181, 'which partitioned Palestine into two states, one Arab, one Jewish ... provides those conditions of international legitimacy that ensure the right of the Palestinian Arab people to sovereignty and national independence'.[13] The Palestinian state would consist of the West Bank and Gaza Strip. In practice, in signing the 1993 DoP and subsequent agreements, the PLO leadership has set its sights still lower, accepting that it will not even achieve statehood in the whole of the 1967 occupied Palestinian territories.

Numerous factors led to the PLO's abandonment of the bold vision of 1969, but they were all bound up, one way or another, with the leadership's perception of the adverse balance of power regionally and internationally. Some argued that the PLO had made a generous offer to Israeli Jews in 1969, but that they rejected it, preferring to keep a Jewish state. The PLO therefore had to re-think its position. How important this factor was is open to question: given the enormous military advantage Israel enjoyed in 1969, the living standards of its people and the realisation of what they would be expected to give up, Palestinian leaders would have had to be pretty naive (which they were not) to believe that a large section of the Israeli public would embrace the notion of a non-sectarian, democratic state of Palestine. Another factor in the PLO's moves to embrace a much more limited aim was its calculation of what it needed to do to win increased international support beyond the Middle East region.

Friends and Enemies

In the late 1960s, the leftists of the PFLP and DFLP identified three enemies of the Palestinian revolution: Zionism, imperialism and Arab reaction. This last always tended to be identified in general terms, according to the state of relations between the Palestinian movement and the Arab regimes. Many in Fatah agreed with the leftist organisations' analysis, but Fatah and the PLO's attempts to establish good relations with all the Arab states and their organisation's standing policy of seeking to avoid becoming entangled in the internal affairs of the Arab states meant that they were much more cautious in pinpointing Arab enemies. As, in the 1970s, the PLO put increasing efforts into seeking Western support, statements about imperialism went on being made, but they had limited practical implications.[14]

Among the Western countries, the PLO and its constituent organisations increasingly distinguished between the United States and other states, which took a more critical position towards Israel and were prepared to uphold at least some of the Palestinians' rights. The US was Israel's main foreign supporter, providing it with generous economic and military assistance and repeatedly vetoing UN resolutions critical of Israel. Palestinians were killed by weapons supplied by the US; those under Israeli occupation knew that US aid, US private donations and the US veto in the UN gave vital support to the Israeli settlement policies which were eating away their control over their lands. Various explanations were advanced to explain the strength of US backing for Israel. The left normally argued that Israel was either a tool or an ally of the United States against movements for liberation and progressive change in the Arab world, while the PLO mainstream (as well as most Palestinians) pointed to the strength of the Zionist lobby in the US as the vital factor.

It was the position which the US took towards the Palestinian people and the PLO which determined their attitude towards it, rather than any deep-rooted ideological rejection of what the US stood for. The PLO was always keen to talk with the US and seek to win support from it, but the stand taken by the US forced it to maintain a public position critical of US policies around the world and to align itself with states and movements hostile to the US.

Pro-Israel lobbyists in the US used the fact of this alignment to portray the PLO as part of Soviet schemes for world domination and thus evade arguments over the specific rights and wrongs of the Palestine issue.

The independent Palestinian organisations had broadly similar views on who were the potential allies of the Palestinian people, although there were significant differences on details. The Arab people/Arab nation was considered to be an ally of the first importance. In spite of the defeat suffered by pan-Arabism in 1967, it was still a major part of the currency of political discourse in the late 1960s and after. The left stressed support from the people in their public statements and built links with revolutionary opposition groups in states under regimes which they identified as 'reactionary', such as Saudi Arabia and Oman. Fatah encouraged popular support while trying to stay on good terms with the existing governments. However, all elements of the Palestinian national movement shared a scepticism about how much could be expected of the Arab regimes. They thought that Arab popular solidarity with the Palestinians, aroused further by admiration for Palestinian resistance activity, could exert pressure on governments to take a more resolute stand in their support. In practice, after the 1960s, as mass support waned and the Arab state system proved more durable and resistant to public pressure than had been anticipated, the Arab policies of all Palestinian organisations were increasingly focused on relations with the existing regimes.

Following the debacle of 1970 in Jordan the PLO lost much of its freedom of action. Its position in Lebanon, the one country where it could still maintain a strong independent presence, was not secure and it needed to perform a continuous balancing act among the Arab states to secure the maximum support for its position without becoming dependent upon any one state. It was recognised as 'the sole legitimate representative of the Palestinian people' at the Rabat summit of Arab heads of state in October 1974, despite Jordanian disquiet.

The PLO as an institution was rapidly absorbed into the Arab state system. Oil-rich Saudi Arabia, Kuwait, Qatar and the United Arab Emirates became regular financial donors and they also helped the PLO by allowing it to collect a tax from Palestinians resident in their territories. This income financed the establishment of a quasi-state structure, the acquisition of arms and the creation of a world-wide network of diplomatic missions. It enabled the PLO to build up social services for the Palestinians in Lebanon, to pay allowances to families who had lost members in the liberation struggle, to channel money to supporters living under Israeli rule to aid their activity and, on occasion, simply to buy support. Its inflated structure and large financial commitments made the PLO reliant on its sources of finance in the Gulf region. Some of this support was given willingly enough (links with Qatar had always been strong), but it had also been a means by which conservative regimes could discourage Palestinian support for oppositionists within their countries. The waning of Arab popular support gave the PLO less leverage upon the oil-rich states, but until 1990, the money kept flowing.

Third World liberation movements were another obvious ally. The PLO developed good relations with some, such as the ANC, at an early date. However, if establishing friendly links with a particular movement would interfere with the realisation of an objective which seemed more important, the PLO did not do so. From at least the mid-1970s onwards, PLO contacts with other liberation movements were largely governed by how they might affect relations with the Arab states and Soviet bloc. Movements which fought against Arab states, such as FPOLISARIO, opposing Morocco in Western Sahara, were ignored or kept at arm's length. Friendly ties existed between the PLO and the Eritrean liberation movement until the overthrow of Haile Selassie in 1974. The new regime soon professed a commitment to socialism and developed strong links with the Soviet Union, which the PLO regarded as a vital ally. At this point, it advised the EPLF to give up its struggle and seek to come to terms with the Ethiopian government, arguing that no liberation movement could succeed without Soviet support.[15] The EPLF ignored the PLO's advice and, adhering to a policy of self-reliance, went on to achieve an independent Eritrea.

The question of the attitude of the 'socialist countries' was a difficult one. In the 1960s, Fatah was wary of the Palestinian cause being turned into an East versus West issue and the PLO, under its leadership, continued to try to persuade world governments to treat Palestine as an issue in its own right, not a detail of the Cold War. Good relations were established with China, then engaged in a fierce political struggle against 'Soviet revisionism', but Fatah and the PLO were careful not to align themselves with China against the Soviet Union, nor did China demand this as a condition for its support.

The PFLP located itself politically among the movements and aligned itself with the states which it saw as having the greatest commitment to revolutionary internationalism, especially Cuba and Vietnam. Only after the early 1970s, as many independent revolutionary movements suffered grave defeats, did the PFLP align itself decisively with the Soviet Union. Much the same was true of the DFLP, whose politics had a Maoist tinge to them at its birth in 1969.[16]

The Soviet Union initially had a negative attitude towards the modern Palestinian national movement. After supporting partition in 1947, it was one of the first states to recognise Israel in 1948. Relations cooled in the 1950s, but the Soviet Union consistently maintained its support for Israel's existence within the borders which it attained in 1949, even after breaking off diplomatic relations with Israel as a result of the 1967 war. It therefore disagreed fundamentally with the reborn Palestinian national movement's aims. Nor did it look too kindly on its armed struggle: for most of the 1960s, national liberation movements which engaged in armed struggle were viewed as a threat to Soviet efforts to ensure peaceful co-existence with the West. In 1970, Soviet support for the plan for a settlement advanced by US Secretary of State William Rogers was criticised indirectly by Palestinian leaders: it took no account of the rights of the Palestinians and it brought an end to the Egypt–Israel 'War of Attrition' along the Suez Canal, thus reducing Arab pressure on Israel.

Relations soon improved. Nasser had arranged the first unofficial contact with the Soviet Union in 1968. The first official visit to Moscow by Yasser Arafat took place in 1972. It is not publicly known how strongly the Soviet Union urged on the PLO the 'two state' solution which it supported, but it does not seem coincidental that the warming of PLO–Soviet relations occurred as the PLO moved towards accepting that as its aim.

The Palestinian movement could call upon support from the Muslim world and Muslim states readily gave diplomatic backing to the Palestinians. At a popular level, the conflict with Israel was usually interpreted in religious terms in Muslim countries outside the Arab world, which does not accord with the views of most Palestinians, who see it in national terms. In the West, the PLO has been careful to emphasise that the conflict in Palestine is not about religion and so has not laid great stress on the significance of Muslim support, welcome as it was.

While the West was overwhelmingly pro-Israel at the time of the 1967 war, the Palestinian organisations hoped to change that. The first contacts were chiefly with groups and activists on the far left, who saw the Palestinian fidai'in as heroic freedom fighters whose cause was just. Solidarity campaigns arose, encouraged by the Palestinian groups. The earliest ones tended to be aligned with Fatah, although there were also pro-PFLP and pro-DPFLP groups:

the PLO was regarded as a bureaucratic apparatus of secondary importance, and that was how it tended to be presented to the solidarity movements by Palestinian activists until four or five years after Fatah had won control. After that, solidarity organisations were encouraged to focus their support on the PLO.[17] The pro-Soviet left was absent from the early solidarity movement. It was only when the Soviet Union gave its seal of approval that the pro-Moscow communist parties were prepared to give their support to solidarity work, although not if it was undertaken by organisations supporting the democratic, non-sectarian state line.

The influence of the early solidarity movement was limited and the PLO switched its main effort to cultivating the support of more 'mainstream' groups and individuals. By the late 1970s, the encouragement of a grassroots movement of solidarity had assumed a very low priority. This change of tack produced useful gains, but has had its negative side. Establishment support has often come with a price tag of pressure for ever more 'moderation', which has not necessarily involved concessions which improved the Palestinians' tactical position vis-a-vis Israel. It is also the case that Palestinian rights did not come high up the list of priorities for most politicians in the West, normally ranking somewhat lower than the capture or retention of office. The development of a strong solidarity movement, in parallel with the quest for establishment support, might have provided a more solid basis for securing a far-reaching change in the positions of Western parties and governments by making it in their interest to adopt a strongly pro-Palestinian position.

In the 1980s, as the PLO pursued a diplomatic strategy to win its goals, it sought to focus solidarity work on diplomatic goals, which sapped the strength of the solidarity movement. Supporters were urged to centre their political demands on an appeal for the Palestine conflict to be resolved through:

> ... the convening of an international peace conference on the Middle East attended by all parties to the conflict, including the representatives of Israel, the Palestine Liberation Organization, those Arab states party to the conflict, the United States and the Soviet Union, under the auspices of the United Nations as called for by the United Nations General Assembly resolution 38/58 C.[18]

The PLO saw this as a demand which had international legitimacy and it certainly hoped that, with the participation of the USSR and the backing of a series of UN resolutions supportive of Palestinian rights, it might achieve success in negotiations with a US-backed Israel. As the rejectionist duo of the US and Israel understood this perfectly well, they would never agree to the convening of such a conference and in the end, all the years of calling for it were so much wasted effort. They came to nothing following the 1990–91 Gulf conflict, when the Madrid peace conference was convened, without UN involvement, under the auspices of the USA and a Soviet Union on the verge of expiring.

The notion of trying to focus the solidarity movement's political demands on the call for the convening of this conference was completely misconceived. It is hard to imagine a call more uninspiring and less capable of raising support on the streets and in workplaces. Solidarity movements are best at building support for clear demands for what, at a popular level, seems just and fair. A call for the Palestinian people to be able to decide their own future in their own country would have been much more readily comprehensible and likely to rally public support: there was nothing to stop the PLO from using that support at the diplomatic level to press for the avenue to peace of its choosing.

The PLO, in line with its diplomatic strategy, has had a strong tendency to argue for Palestinian rights by reference to UN resolutions which uphold them, such as Resolution 194. Many are indeed supportive of the Palestinian position, but at the level of building popular solidarity, such resolutions carry less weight than people's own general sense of right and wrong: they think that Palestinian refugees should be able to go back to their country because they feel that everyone has a right to live in their own country. They would think that irrespective of whether the UN had passed a resolution on the subject.

The stress on the diplomatic strategy does not alone explain the PLO's approach. Underlying it has been a lack of appreciation of how public opinion is mobilised and makes itself felt in the West. Operating in a Middle East environment in which undemocratic regimes intolerant of dissent are the norm and independent media and non-governmental organisations are far weaker than in the West, this is perhaps not too surprising. What is less justifiable was its reluctance to learn.

Armed Struggle

Fatah had strongly affirmed that armed struggle was the only way to liberate Palestine and this was written into the Palestine

National Charter in 1968 as Fatah wished. The PFLP, DFLP and other Palestinian groups which emerged in the 1960s shared this view. Yet in spite of their unequivocal declarations, the role of armed struggle within Palestinian strategy varied a great deal and was only central to it for a relatively short period of time.

The Palestinians in the ANM considered that the political basis for waging armed struggle had not been laid at the time when Fatah carried out its first operation, but from Fatah's viewpoint, it accomplished what it was meant to do:

> Above all, we wanted to mount a spectacular operation that would arrest the attention of the Israelis, Palestinians, Arab regimes, and world public opinion. We wanted to signal our presence to the Israelis, reinforce the Palestinians' determination to fight on their own, challenge the Arab regimes, and remind the world of the fate of our people.[19]

Fatah attracted growing support from Palestinians who contrasted its militant activity with the rhetorical militancy (unaccompanied by action) of the newly founded PLO. Following the June 1967 war, the relaunching of the armed struggle in August was less significant for the damage it inflicted upon Israel than for the political impact it had, especially upon Palestinians. The great groundswell of support for the fidai'in after Karameh created problems as well as great opportunities. Thousands of raw but enthusiastic volunteers had to be trained militarily and educated politically, but this imposed an enormous strain on organisations whose existing membership was far outnumbered by the new recruits.

Another difficulty was created by the proliferation of 'fidai'in organisations' which now took place. Some were genuinely independent Palestinian resistance organisations, such as the DPFLP and the PFLP-General Command, both of which split from the PFLP, but others, such as Saiqa and the Arab Liberation Front, were creations of Arab regimes. Some were set up by individuals who simply could not bear to serve in the lower ranks of other organisations. There were up to 30 supposed 'fidai'in organisations' in 1970, many unaccountable to the Palestinian people in any way and whose main activity seemed to consist of issuing grandiloquent communiques. The defeat of the movement in Jordan caused most of the micro-groups to vanish, but the Palestinian liberation movement remained far more splintered than its counterparts anywhere else in the world. This made it more difficult to agree upon common PLO policies – a problem further complicated by the fact that, at PNC meetings, participating organisations made a principle of achieving unanimity between groups. The first major departure from this practice only occurred in 1988, when the PFLP voted against the major policy statements (mainly because they accepted the UN partition resolution of 1947 as a political basis for declaring a Palestinian state), but did not seek to stop them being passed by demanding unanimity. A third problem for the long term was that the national movement outside Palestine was transformed virtually overnight from one operating in semi-clandestinity in the neighbouring Arab countries into an overwhelmingly 'overground' movement, more vulnerable to infiltration by agents of hostile intelligence activities and to repression.

Fatah advanced a coherent strategy,[20] involving the mobilisation of Palestinians inside and outside the occupied homeland in a guerrilla struggle which would impose an increasing strain on Israel. This, allied with the winning of international political support, would eventually create conditions in which the Palestinians could achieve their goals. As the liberation movement's armed strength was overwhelmingly concentrated outside Palestine, it needed to be able to strike repeatedly at Israel from neighbouring Arab states. If Israel was thereby forced to concentrate its forces on the borders, this would help those organising internal resistance.

In 1968–70, the PLO succeeded in opening up two Arab fronts to Palestinian commando action – in Jordan and Lebanon. The Syrian front remained closed to Palestinian operations, although Syria helped with communications and training facilities. Egypt's 'War of Attrition' along the Suez Canal activated another important Arab front, which certainly served to pin down Israeli forces. A small part of Fatah's strategic vision was therefore realised. However, it had crucially underestimated the disparity in strength between the two sides and overestimated its ability to mobilise armed action within Palestine. The impact of fidai'in attacks declined as Israel implemented effective counter-measures: fences, mines and regular patrols on the Lebanese and Jordanian borders, air raids, shelling and occasional assaults on the ground, directed at hitting the fidai'in and provoking hostility towards them among local civilians made to pay a price for their presence.

In the West Bank, such guerrilla cells as were established from time to time were soon caught or killed. The resistance in the Gaza Strip, led by the PFLP, was cut off by sea and land from direct external support: collective punishments, the driving of broad roads through refugee camps to allow easy access, the operations of assassination squads and the use of all the means of counter-insurgency that Israel could muster crushed the guerrilla movement there in 1971. The fact that the first years of the occupation saw a rise in living standards as a result of the rapid expansion of employment in Israel also worked against the guerrillas. Crucially, while local people generally admired the guerrillas, most were not prepared to take the risks involved in giving them shelter and practical assistance: they had too much to lose. The strength of the resistance in the refugee camps of the Gaza Strip can be seen as not only a tribute to the activists of the PFLP, but also a product of the material conditions in which their inhabitants lived: they were those who had the least to lose.

Even before their defeat in Jordan in September 1970, it was becoming clear that the armed struggle was turning into little more than a series of increasingly suicidal raids across the ceasefire lines. Communiques made claims of heavy casualties inflicted upon the enemy, but they bore little semblance to reality. The fidai'in fell into the propaganda habits of Arab states, upon which they had once poured scorn. Following 'Black September' and the suppression of the Palestinian guerrilla movement in Jordan, only the much shorter Israel–Lebanon border remained open to fidai'in operations.

From this point on, however much lip service was paid to the armed struggle as a strategy, armed actions became a tactic for the entire Palestinian resistance movement. The actions of the Black September group, which announced its existence with the assassination of Jordanian Prime Minister Wasfi Tal in November 1971, are a case in point. It soon turned from Jordanian targets to Israeli and 'imperialist' ones. It shocked the world when it seized members of the Israeli team at the 1972 Munich Olympics, who it said would be released in exchange for the freedom of Palestinian prisoners. No exchange took place and the hostages were killed during a shoot-out with German soldiers at Munich airport. Israel responded to Black September attacks by assassinating PLO officials supposedly working with the group and with more raids on alleged guerrilla positions.

What is known of those involved in Black September indicates that most of its operatives were Fatah members and that its leadership came from within Fatah: it has been claimed that it was led by Abu Iyad.[21] Its attacks evidently did not represent a strategic option. They were a product of their time. In the wake of the expulsion of the fidai'in from Jordan, when the Palestinians were in a much weaker political position, Black September attacks served as a warning to those in the Arab world suspected of willingness to take part in a 'capitulationist' settlement which disregarded the rights of the Palestinians. Ironically, when Egypt and Syria went to war against Israel in October 1973 to recover the lands they lost in 1967, it ultimately led to Palestinian fears being partially realised: but for the trauma of that war, Israel would not have been ready to give up Sinai as the price of a separate peace treaty with Egypt in 1979.

Subsequent Fatah operations were clearly tactical, not part of a continuing strategy of armed struggle. An example was that which took place on 11 March 1978, when Fatah commandos landed on the Israeli coast with the mission of taking a group of Israeli soldiers hostage to exchange for imprisoned Palestinians. It went badly wrong, resulting in a shoot-out in which 31 Israelis (many of them passengers on a hijacked bus) and six Palestinians were killed. The operation took place four months after Sadat went to Jerusalem to launch Egypt–Israel peace negotiations and was intended 'to show Israel that it was futile to exclude us from a settlement and remind the Arabs that it was dangerous to sacrifice us to their selfish interests'.[22]

The same trend occurred in the operations of other groups, notably the PFLP. Since the mid-1980s, if not before, PFLP operations have had the appearance of being actions designed to affirm to the Palestinian public that the Front still offers a more militant alternative to Fatah, rather than actions forming part of any serious strategy of armed struggle. On 11 December 1996, members of the PFLP carried out a drive-by shooting of a group of settlers near Ramallah, killing a mother and child. Supposedly a gesture of protest against the continuing occupation and settlement construction, it was neatly timed to happen on the anniversary of the PFLP's foundation. This was 'armed struggle' as a party trick.

In fact, what the smaller Palestinian groups could achieve was very much limited by Fatah's hegemony in the national movement and Fatah, after the defeat in Jordan, was looking for other means than armed struggle to try to change the balance of forces in the Palestinians' favour in their conflict with Israel – primarily, to diplomacy. Occasional armed attacks could raise Palestinian morale, impose a heavy security burden on Israel and send signals out to the rest of the world about the disruptive potential of the Palestinians if no settlement was achieved which took full account of their rights. They were not the principal means by which Fatah or the PLO hoped to realise their aims, but supplemented diplomacy.

This was the true significance of the PLO forces in Lebanon, which Israel's 1982 invasion of that country was intended to crush once and for all. They were important not so much for any armed operations which they conducted against Israel as for the fact that their presence helped to maintain the PLO as a credible independent political force in the region. This was well appreciated by Israel's Defence Minister, Ariel Sharon, and his collaborators in the plan for the assault on Lebanon. The attack was known as 'Operation Peace for Galilee' but Galilee had had eleven months of peace before it started, thanks to the July 1981 US-brokered cease-fire agreement between Israel and the PLO covering the Lebanese border, which the PLO had kept. It was ostensibly a reaction to the Palestinian assassination attempt on Shlomo Argov, Israel's ambassador in London, but that was carried out by the fiercely anti-Arafat group led by Abu Nidal, which had never been part of the PLO. In fact, the attack was intended to destroy the PLO, whose very existence served to encourage Palestinian resistance inside the 1967 occupied territories. There, Israel was vainly attempting to foist the Quisling 'Village Leagues' on the people as a leadership with which it could conclude the autonomy agreement envisaged in its peace treaty with Egypt – an agreement which would confer very limited self-government on the Palestinians of the West Bank and Gaza Strip but allow Israel to retain control over their territory.[23]

The Palestinian forces in Lebanon fought bravely, along with their Lebanese allies, but they were overwhelmed by the weight of the Israeli attack. Forced to leave Beirut at the end of August 1982, the PLO had only limited success in re-establishing a presence in Lebanon, opposed as it was by Syria and most Lebanese political forces. In the 1970s, the Palestinian armed forces had become a bargaining chip in the PLO's diplomatic strategy: the loss of their Lebanese base meant that this chip was taken out of play.

Forced to establish its new headquarters in Tunis, the bulk of its armed forces scattered about the Arab world in enforced, demoralising idleness, its member organisations at odds with each other, the PLO's future did not look hopeful. Although its leaders would not admit as much in public, it was reduced, Micawber-like, to hoping that something would turn up. If that hadn't happened, the PLO might well have faced the same fate as the Arab Higher Committee, consigned to irrelevancy after 1948. But in 1987, something did turn up.

The Intifada

An Israeli truck collided with two vans carrying Palestinian labourers returning to the Gaza Strip from working in Israel. Four Palestinians were killed and seven injured. Rumours spread that this was not an accident, but a deliberate attempt to kill Palestinians. The following day, 9 December 1987, young stone-throwing Palestinians clashed with Israeli soldiers in Jabalya refugee camp, near Gaza City; 15-year-old Hatem al-Sisi was shot dead, the first 'martyr' in the Intifada. Demonstrations rapidly spread throughout the Gaza Strip and West Bank. They became mass confrontations with the occupation forces whose violent reaction failed to suppress them. Something new, something astonishing was happening in Palestine.

The Intifada was a spontaneous popular uprising, neither planned nor anticipated by the PLO or the Islamic organisations which were starting to play a more prominent role in Palestine. It took them by surprise, as well as Israel, which found itself in the unaccustomed position of being placed on the defensive by the Palestinians. The people living under occupation had simply had enough of their treatment at Israel's hands. At the forefront of the street protests were young Palestinians who had grown up under Israeli occupation, witnessing parents humiliated at check-points and in searches, seeing an alien army on their streets and certain that they had nothing to look forward to while the occupation continued. Many felt they had nothing to lose, and that partially explains the fearlessness which many older Palestinians said that they displayed.

A popular uprising does not last long on a spontaneous basis. To sustain revolt, leadership and organisation are required. Both were forthcoming, thanks to the work done by Palestinian organisations within the West Bank and Gaza Strip over the previous ten years or so. After the defeat of the post-1967 war attempts to launch a sustained armed struggle, the focus of activity for the Palestinian national movement shifted towards political mobilisation around issues such as the rejection of King Hussein of Jordan's March 1972 proposals for a United Arab Kingdom (a federated state including both banks of the Jordan), and the mayoral elections of 1972 and 1976. Palestinians responded to PLO calls to protest, but these activities did not encourage much initiative or self-organisation.

This started to be rectified in the late 1970s, with the development of sectoral organisations. Activity around social questions was dominated by established charitable organisations, religious bodies (including some within which the Muslim Brotherhood, parent organisation of Hamas, worked) and the communists (especially in the trade unions). The PLO groups had not seen such work as important when they were concentrating on the armed struggle, but they now began to recognise a potential for building support through activity in the social sphere. They had succeeded in recruiting activists among the intelligentsia inside Palestine and it was mainly from among ex-students, lecturers, teachers, doctors and those with a similar social status that most of the organisers came.

In 1978, supporters of the DFLP established the Palestinian Federation of Women's Action Committees (now known as the Union of Women's Work Committees). Among other activities, it held meetings, organised kindergartens and creches so that women could go out to do paid work and sold products made by women to give them an independent income. Two years later, the communists established the Union of Working Women's Committees, which was followed by the creation of the Fatah-aligned Association of Women's Committees for Social Work and, finally, the PFLP-sympathising Union of Palestinian Women's Committees. All carried on broadly similar activities.

The same pattern occurred in other sectors: each organisation sought to establish groups aligned with itself. Popular medical and agricultural aid organisations were set up: the communist-backed ones were the most successful. The trade unions in the West Bank were united in one federation at first, but when Fatah failed to displace the communist leadership, it split it in two. DFLP sympathisers established the Workers' Unity Bloc and the PFLP, last off the blocks again, established some individual unions.

These organisations set out to meet real needs and some were quite successful at a local level. At the same time, they provided spheres of activity within which supporters of the different Palestinian political factions could gain organising experience and mobilise broader support. A big difficulty with them was that they were obviously faction-based and not broad organisations in which Palestinians of all viewpoints could participate and stand for election. Each group wanted organisations under its political control, rather than broader organisations within which they would seek to win support by argument and example. This necessarily limited their appeal: many Palestinians had a distaste for factional politics which the years have only increased.

In spite of such weaknesses, the sectoral organisations produced activists, experienced organisers and social as well as political networks spreading throughout the 1967 occupied territories. These came into their own when the Intifada erupted. Those who had acquired their skills in the sectoral organisations took part in forming local popular committees to organise strikes, arrange food supplies, help those in greatest need, support prisoners and their families and other undertakings.

An important element in allowing the sectoral organisations to emerge and in giving the Intifada its strength was the changes which had taken place as a result of the years of Israeli occupation. The sweeping success of PLO supporters in the 1976 mayoral elections signalled not only a political transformation, but the rise to power of another generation. The circumstances of the occupation tended to enhance the role of younger people: those who could bring in money from long days of labouring in Israel (as about 150,000 workers did in the years immediately before the Intifada) were overwhelmingly young and middle-aged men. Those from families which had formerly earned most of their income from farming would normally contribute the lion's share of their income if they were able to work regularly in Israel. Political activity and violent resistance were also primarily domains of the middle aged and young. Old people retained social respect, but there was a certain redistribution of power, mainly by common consent, among the generations.

While Israel kept at its disposal the legal and practical means to suppress all but the most clandestine political activity, it was generally selective in how it used them. This was an intelligent policy, as it meant that Palestinians were less cautious about giving away their political connections and revealing networks of contacts by, for example, socialising with people who shared the same political viewpoint or talking carelessly on the telephone without heed as to who might be listening. However, it also meant that there was a certain scope for the expression of divergent political opinions, which could take place in social gatherings, in the East Jerusalem press and, most openly, in the students' unions of the Palestinian universities, where debate was free and elections were democratic. New universities opened during the years of Israeli occupation[24] and these tended to produce graduates who were politically minded, relatively tolerant of divergent views and not hidebound by traditional power structures.

These factors helped to make Palestinian society in the West Bank and Gaza Strip more open and pluralistic than it had been and made its political activists more respectful of each others' strengths and qualities than was often the case with their counterparts in exile, where organisational hierarchies and divisions tended to be more rigid. They also made it more flexible, liberated initiative, created more 'know-how' and fostered national unity across divides of clan, region (of steadily declining significance in any case) and political organisation.

An important contribution to the Intifada's outbreak and persistence was made by the PLO's member organisations when they managed to reunite under the PLO umbrella in 1987 after more than four years of bitter dispute. The signing of a joint declaration in Prague on 6 September 1986 by Fatah, DFLP and Palestinian Communist Party (PCP) representatives offered the first clear sign that the independent Palestinian organisations were on their way to resolving the issues which had divided them. After several other meetings had passed off successfully (including the congress of the Palestinian Writers and Journalists Union and a joint International Women's Day celebration in Jerusalem by the four main women's organisations), the 18th Palestine National Council convened in Algiers on 28 April 1987, at which all but the groups aligned with Syria were represented. It was able to adopt agreed common political positions. Had the major PLO organisations still been in fierce dispute with each other at the end of 1987, it is probable that the Intifada would not have broken out and if it had, it would have collapsed quickly because of political divisions.

A further contribution made to the progress of the Intifada by the PLO organisations consisted of what they refrained from doing. Hitherto, the relationship between the interior and exterior had been extremely unequal. The PLO was recognised as representing the Palestinian people as a whole, and the externally-based leaderships of each constituent organisation were regarded as the overall national authorities within them. The internal organisation was always expected to toe the line set by the national organisation in each case, with little or no room for flexibility to allow for the very different conditions under which it worked. Veteran leaders tended to regard signs of initiative with suspicion. In spite of this, when the Intifada broke out, PLO leaders demonstrated an uncharacteristic lightness of touch in their relations with their internal organisations. A much more equal relationship prevailed.

A United National Leadership of the Uprising (UNLU) was established by the four main PLO groupings inside Palestine (Fatah, PFLP, DFLP and PCP). It issued its first communique on 8 January 1988, after which they appeared in a steady stream until the end of the Intifada, normally roughly at two-week intervals. They were produced in leaflet form and slid under doors, pasted on walls or handed out by activists throughout the West Bank and Gaza Strip. They commented on current events, set forth Palestinian demands and called for actions by Palestinians, particularly strike days. Their importance was clear to all. They were prepared by the UNLU in consultation with the PLO leadership abroad. This showed the limits to the initiative allowed to the internal leaders: they could not simply act on the basis of the known political positions of the PLO, but had to consult with the external leadership about the political statements and demands they made. Security came second to this requirement: exchanges over the texts of UNLU communiques took place via fax machines and telephones, so that Israel had a pretty good idea of who the UNLU leaders were and what their next communique would demand.

The Intifada was the greatest struggle mounted within their homeland by the Palestinians since the 1936–39 revolt. It brought into action women and young people on a scale unknown before in Palestine. As an energetic mass movement, it probably lasted between 18 months and two years, after which it lost momentum and tended to settle into something of a routine sustained by organisation and UNLU calls, finally petering out in 1992.[25]

The Uprising showed the world that the Palestinian people as a whole absolutely rejected Israel's occupation of the West Bank and Gaza Strip. It shook the Israeli occupation regime, had a demoralising effect on the army and made ruling the West Bank and Gaza Strip cost Israel money (instead of being a net income yielder). The majority of Israeli political leaders (not only those of the Zionist left) were forced to recognise that the existing relationship between Israel and the Palestinians would have to change, although for most, this meant seeking a way of perpetuating overall Israeli control without having to deploy Israeli soldiers throughout Palestinian residential areas in order to do it.

A more negative side to the Intifada emerged as the strength of popular participation waned. In the early months of the Uprising, collaborators had been given the chance to repent and make their peace with their people, which severely damaged the Shin Bet's network of informers. Those who continued to collaborate could expect little mercy and, as mass participation declined somewhat, killings of alleged collaborators rose. The UNLU and PLO made some effort to severely limit such killings because of their propaganda value to Israel and because they remembered their results in the 1936–39 revolt. As the revolutionary impulse faded and economic conditions deteriorated, Palestinian society tended to seek refuge in more conservative social values. Whereas the first couple of years were marked by a high level of women's activism, there came setbacks later on. Women found themselves under pressure to conform to traditional behavioural norms, especially in the historically more conservative regions, where Hamas' efforts to impose its version of Islamic values enjoyed wider social acceptance and frequently found a passive response from the PLO groups.[26]

Political gains from the Intifada might have been greater but for events which took place far from Palestine's borders. The Soviet bloc crumbled away during the first three years of the Intifada, knocking out one of the pillars of the PLO's diplomatic strategy. Then, in August 1990, President Saddam Hussein of Iraq sent the Iraqi army into Kuwait and annexed it. In the ensuing conflict between Iraq and the US-led coalition which aimed to turf it out of Kuwait, there was no doubt where the sympathies of the vast majority of Palestinians lay. Wishful thinking seemed to prevail over common sense; there was a widespread belief that Iraq would win. When the air war began, credence was given to wildly exaggerated Iraqi claims of coalition airplanes downed; once the truth that the coalition had total control of the skies had sunk in, many clung to the belief that the Iraqi army would perform well in the ground war. Its comprehensive rout came as another shock.

The consequences of having taken this attitude were catastrophic. The Arab states of the Gulf took their revenge on the Palestinians by cutting off financial support to the PLO and expelling the great majority of their Palestinian residents, most of whom had not shared their compatriots' enthusiasm for the Iraqi dictator. As these communities had given generously to the PLO and were often sending money to support families in the West Bank, Gaza Strip, Jordan, Syria or Lebanon, this was a devastating double blow. Conditions deteriorated rapidly for millions of Palestinians. The PLO could not operate as before: an elaborate structure built and maintained over more than 20 years and dependent upon generous infusions of Arab oil money began to disintegrate. Families of martyrs found the financial support they had previously received drying up; money which the PLO had dispensed to its constituent organisations was no longer forthcoming, so their own institutions went into crisis; PLO offices, established as the result of efforts which had brought the PLO wider diplomatic relations than the State of Israel in the 1980s, one by one closed down except for those regarded as the most important. In addition, some public sympathy was temporarily lost in the West: the Palestinians were seen to have taken a hypo-critical stance of wanting human rights and self-determination for themselves, while supporting a dictator who denied them to Kuwaitis and Kurds, besides treating many Iraqi Arabs in the most brutal way.

Palestinian reasons for supporting Iraq in the Gulf crisis varied. They included resentment towards oil rich states which Palestinians felt should do more to support them, and sympathy for Saddam Hussein because he had made statements declaring his determination to stand up to Israel at a time when the rest of the Arab world appeared to prefer a supine posture. The main motivation seems to have been opposition to Western (especially US) action against fellow Arabs. Because they had seen the United States arm Israel, bolster its economy and shield it against international efforts to make it respect Palestinian rights and disgorge the territories it occupied in 1967, opposition to action in the Arab world by the USA came naturally. Some Palestinians (still very much a minority) have since concluded that their stand in the Gulf crisis was mistaken, but even they are divided between those who think it was wrong in principle and the ones who simply regard it as a tactical error.

The PLO had, at the outset, criticised Iraq's invasion of Kuwait and called for a negotiated solution to the crisis, but aligned itself with Iraq in opposing the US-led coalition. On this occasion, there was no doubt that it was in tune with Palestinian popular feeling. It would have been wiser not to have been and to have tried to inject a bit of realism into the popular mood, but it shared in the illusions and sentiments of the people. Had it built its demands for Palestinian rights on universal principles rather than an appeal to specific UN resolutions favouring the Palestinians, it might have kept its bearings better in this crisis and taken a stand that was not only more principled, but tactically advantageous too.

The Intifada had rescued the PLO leadership from marginalisation and strengthened its hand in pursuing diplomatic gains for the Palestinian cause: Jordan had officially relinquished all claim to the West Bank and the USA had even been induced to open a direct dialogue with it for a few months. As the dust of the Gulf War settled, it found itself facing similar challenges to those confronting it before the Intifada, but was more poorly equipped to meet them. The Soviet bloc had vanished and some powerful Arab states were angry with the PLO, severely undercutting its diplomatic strategy. The PLO's 'state in waiting' apparatus was collapsing under the impact of financial crisis, but to make matters worse, the leadership was far weaker. Israeli assassination had taken a toll of experienced Palestinian leaders during the previous 25 years, but at the beginning of the Intifada, three of Fatah's founders – Yasser Arafat, Abu Jihad and Abu Iyad – still stood at the head of the PLO. Abu Jihad, deputy military commander, was assassinated in his home in Tunis in a Mossad/army operation on 16 April 1988, four months after the Intifada broke out. Abu Iyad, head of security and an influential political voice, was gunned down by a member of the anti-PLO group led by Abu Nidal (and long sponsored by Iraq) on 14 January 1991, hours before the expiry of the UN ultimatum to Iraq to withdraw from Kuwait. The death of these veterans deprived the PLO of leaders who had wielded considerable authority in their own right and whose opinions carried great weight with Arafat, whose tendency to concentrate power in his own hands and make policy decisions without prior reference to the responsible PLO bodies became virtually unrestrained, save only by his sense of what the Palestinians would accept.

Arafat's own health was deteriorating. With events seeming to conspire against him and the organisation he headed, he accepted the terms imposed upon the Palestinians as a precondition for their participation in the Madrid Middle East peace conference in 1991. When the talks which followed became bogged down, he engaged in secret diplomacy without the consent or knowledge of the PLO's leading bodies to agree terms for a settlement with Israel. This was the background to the ceremony which took place on the White House lawn on 13 September 1993, when Rabin and Arafat signed the Declaration of Principles.

4

A New Stage?

The agreements reached between Israel and the PLO in 1993 brought to an end the era of Palestinian history which had opened with the revival of the national movement, spearheaded by Fatah, in the 1960s. Like the first phase of the Palestinian conflict with Zionism, this one too draws to a close in defeat: there is no other term for an outcome which falls so far short of what the modern Palestinian resistance movement set out to achieve.[1]

The Palestinian opponents of the deals struck between Israel and Yasser Arafat made forceful criticisms of it, but suffered from the critical weakness of being unable to offer a convincing alternative. The PFLP and DFLP denounced the DoP, but what have they offered in its place? To oppose the 'DoP', they formed an alliance with all the other Palestinian groups who were against it, including Hamas. Hamas did not need them: it was powerful enough inside Palestine to pursue its own strategy vis-a-vis the Palestinian National Authority established as a result of the DoP; all they did was to compromise the secular principles in which many of their members and supporters strongly believed. With nowhere else to go, they drifted towards playing the part of a loyal opposition to the PNA.

Nor do the Islamic movements offer a real alternative. At moments of deep Palestinian frustration at the 'peace process', Hamas bombings in Israel have won it some support, but they do not offer a way forward for the Palestinian struggle. Had Hamas confined its attacks to striking at Israeli soldiers and settlers in the West Bank and Gaza Strip, it might have had an impact in encouraging an Israeli withdrawal, but by carrying out bomb attacks within Israel against civilians, it has sent a message to Israelis that they are not secure anywhere, whoever they are. This only encourages them to vote for those who pledge to be 'tough on security' and by denying them Israel as a place of safety, gives soldiers and settlers less motivation to get out. In circumstances in which all Israeli Jews believe their survival to be at stake, Israel will stop at nothing to counter the threat. Anyone entertaining the notion that a war of attrition, people against people, Muslims against Jews, can bring about a Palestinian victory is very much mistaken. In each conflict since the 1930s, the ratio of Palestinian Arab to Jewish/Israeli losses has nearly always been in the order of ten to one or higher, and Israel has the power to raise it much more: Palestine will run out of Palestinians before Israel runs out of Jews, to put it bluntly.

If a simple reversion to older strategies of armed struggle or the newer version practised by Hamas doesn't offer a way forward for the Palestinians, do they have any options left, other than surrender to the dictates of the Israeli government? In a short survey which cannot do justice to a huge subject, I have tried to show how the conflict between the Palestinians and Zionism developed as one between two societies. The society which Zionism created in Palestine was simply far stronger than that of the people who already lived there when modern political Zionism was born. The fact that those who founded the Zionist movement and devoted tireless effort to the creation of the State of Israel were Jewish is important in explaining why they undertook such a formidable challenge, but much less so in explaining how they achieved most of their aims. The crucial factor was that they came from European societies. They could draw on political skills, experience of political mobilisation, diplomatic expertise, education, scientific knowledge, financial resources, understanding of modern bureaucratic systems and other elements of a civilisation which, in the nineteenth century, dominated the world. To express the same point another way, they could utilise the products of a hundred years and more of political revolution and reform, industrialisation and the rise to global ascendency of Western capitalism. It is true that most of those who settled in Palestine before 1948 came from the more backward regions of Europe, but even so, the resources (in the broadest sense) upon which they could draw far exceeded those of the Palestinian Arabs, particularly as they formed part of a movement which also had a strong body of supporters in the most advanced capitalist countries.

The Palestinian Arabs, like other peoples in Asia, Africa, Australasia and the Americas in earlier times, had a society which functioned well enough when left to itself, but it was ill-adapted to withstand a determined assault from Europe. The advantages the Palestinians had in numbers and possession of the land at the beginning of the century might have been enough to outweigh those possessed by the colonists (as they ultimately were in Algeria, Zimbabwe and South Africa) but, following Hitler's rise to power in Europe and the consequent upsurge in Jewish immigration to Palestine, the Jewish population passed the critical point at which the Zionist movement gained an absolute advantage over the Palestinians. The outcome of the conflict was not inevitable: a less astute leadership in the Yishuv, a Palestinian national movement which made fewer mistakes, a decision by other European powers to stand firm against Nazi Germany at an earlier date and perhaps precipitate Hitler's fall: many factors could have shifted the balance of power one way or the other.

The state for which the Zionist movement fought came into being in 1948. In it emerged an Israeli Jewish nation. Wealthy in individuals of knowledge and skill, the new state, with its power to marshal and direct resources, developed industry, agriculture, the institutions of democracy and a system of universal education, with advanced research bodies, as well as formidable armed forces and intelligence services. These opened up an ever wider disparity between the power of Israel and that of the Palestinians, which the modern Palestinian national movement has tried to overcome by bringing into play the strength of other states.

Palestinian society changed a lot after 1948. It produced a revitalised national movement which helped to unite Palestinians as a people across all the borders which separated them. That movement's achievements were considerable – a fact which its present state should not be allowed to obscure. It played no small part in making the Palestinians a people with a strong sense of their national identity, educated, politicised and still confident in the justice of their national cause.

If one chapter in the history of the relationship between Israeli Jews and Palestinian Arabs is drawing to a close, it is not at all obvious what might follow. What is clear is that the Palestinians still have a long way to go before they secure their rights. Israeli and Palestinian societies are continuing to evolve and the way in which they change will inevitably have an impact on the future evolution of the relations between the two peoples. Since the 1980s, Israelis have become more individualistic, more concerned with their personal interests and those of their families, and less inclined to make sacrifices for the 'national interest'. They are less ideologically driven: they get on with their lives without a burning sense that they are undertaking a historic mission. The difference is seen in gradual changes in attitudes towards army service, in the steady erosion of the collectivist values of the kibbutz and in the growing pragmatism of the centre ground of Israeli politics. This does make a difference to how Israelis think about peace with the

Palestinians: the majority are concerned about personal security, being able to go about their lives normally and earn a living and they don't have a commitment to controlling the whole 'Land of Israel', maintaining settlements in the heart of the West Bank and Gaza Strip or even to maintaining exclusive Israeli sovereignty over Jerusalem. That was why, when Likud leader Netanyahu campaigned for votes in 1996, he conducted a deceptive campaign: though ideologically opposed to the DoP and to giving up full Israeli control over the West Bank, he stressed the security issue.

At the same time, Israel is a divided society and some of those divisions are worsening. They won't bring about Israel's self-destruction, but they have implications for Israel's relations with the Palestinians – including those who are its citizens. In Israeli Jewish society, the parties of the right have a majority because they have been successful in winning the great majority of the Oriental Jewish vote and most of the religious section of the population supports chauvinistic religious parties. Relations between the religious and non-religious sectors of the population are deteriorating. Privatisation and economic reform in Israel since the 1980s have greatly increased the gap between rich and poor: the disparities in 1990s Israel are among the largest in the developed world. As the Labour Party led the way in pushing economic reform and Oriental Jews were disproportionately concentrated in the lower strata of Israeli society, this only reinforced their alienation from it.

The Palestinians are more fragmented geographically than ever. Many Palestinians living outside their homeland feel that they have been abandoned by the leadership which they supported, often with their blood, for a quarter of a century. Those in the West Bank and Gaza Strip were glad to see Israeli troops leave their cities, but are appalled at the corruption and violations of human rights which take place under the Palestinian National Authority. For these reasons, many Palestinians are becoming more individualistic, concentrating on the interests of those dearest to them and putting to the back of their minds the dreams they once had for Palestine. If they don't like the way the PNA is going, they don't see convincing alternatives.

This won't last. The talents, knowledge, courage and determination which the Palestinian people have in abundance will give rise to a third wave of Palestinian resistance. If a new movement in some shape or form learns well from its people's past, then it may be one through which the Palestinians finally achieve a peace which may not render them their full measure of justice – that is now impossible – but with which they can be content. It will still face the challenge of the disparity in strength between the Palestinian people and Israel and will need to find ways of redressing the balance. Seeking to build support for the Palestinian cause around the world, including among the American public, will be vital, but so will a rewriting of the terms of this conflict. The Palestinians need to find ways to ally with all that is enlightened in Israel against what is racist and repressive. This does not mean sweeping the past under the carpet, or pretending that fundamental disagreements don't continue to exist. It does mean recognising that a new *modus vivendi* has to be found to allow two peoples, long engaged in conflict, to co-exist in peace and equality in the land which is now home to both.

Notes

Introduction

1. An eyewitness account by Israeli writer Amos Keinan of the expulsion of the villagers was published in English in *Israel Imperial News* (London, March 1968).
2. The Deir Yassin massacre is described or mentioned in practically all general accounts of the Palestine conflict and works specifically dealing with the events of 1948. It is the only massacre by Jewish forces normally mentioned in mainstream Zionist historical works on this period: it was well publicised, it was carried out by the Irgun Zvai Leumi and LEHI rightist minority groups, rather than the mainstream Haganah, and was condemned by their political rivals in the Jewish Agency. Most sources put the Palestinian death toll at around 250, but study undertaken by the Research and Documentation Centre of Bir Zeit University suggests a figure of 170 is more accurate.
3. The Declaration of Principles and its annexes were published in the *Palestinian–Israeli Peace Agreement – A Documentary Record* (Washington: Institute for Palestine Studies, 1993). Subsequent agreements have been published and negotiations chronicled by the *Journal of Palestine Studies* (University of California Press: hereafter, '*JPS*') in its 'Documents and Source Material' and 'Peace Monitor' sections. On developments in Palestine since the signing of the Declaration of Principles, see Graham Usher, *Palestine in Crisis* (London and East Haven: Pluto Press/TNI/MERIP, 1995), the weekly *Palestine Report* (Jerusalem Media and Communication Centre, Jerusalem) and the *JPS*.

1. Independence and Catastrophe

1. Edward Said's *The Question of Palestine* (London: Vintage, 1992) is perhaps the best known.

2. Good examples are *All That Remains* (ed. Walid Khalidi, Washington: Institute for Palestine Studies, 1992), which documents the Palestinian villages destroyed by Israel in 1948 and after, Nur Masalha, *Expulsion of the Palestinians: The Concept of 'Transfer' in Zionist Political Thought, 1882–1948* (Washington: Institute for Palestine Studies, 1992) and Rashid Khalidi, *Palestinian Identity – The Construction of Modern National Consciousness* (New York: Columbia University Press, 1997).

3. Studies on topics such as the Israeli economy, the Histadrut and the kibbutz were published by the PLO Research Centre between 1965 and 1969.

4. Yasser Arafat spoke of Neturei Karta when he addressed South African Muslims in Johannesburg on 10 May 1994:

    We are not against the Jews. We must remember what the Qur'an says: 'Within the people of Moses there is a nation that believes in Justice and lives by it.' For your information, there are two Jewish sects in Palestine: the Samaritans in Nablus and the Neturey Karta in Jerusalem. They refuse to recognise the State of Israel and regard themselves as Palestinians. I am saying this to prove that their [Israel's – my note] statements that Jerusalem is their capital are wrong. (*JPS*, No. 23, Autumn 1994, p. 132)

5. *Basic Political Documents of the Armed Palestinian Resistance Movement* (ed. Leila S. Kadi, Beirut: PLO Research Centre, 1969, p. 140).

6. *The Palestine National Liberation Movement, Al Fateh* (Undated pamphlet, but evidently published in 1969 or 1970 in Amman, p. 4).

7. *A Strategy for the Liberation of Palestine* (Adopted by the PFLP at its First Congress. Amman: PFLP Information Department, 1969, p. 78).

8. Ibid., p. 80.

9. The Charter of Hamas was published in *JPS*, No. 88, Summer, 1993.

10. The question of the relationship between Israeli identity and Jewish identity is discussed in, among other publications, Akiva Orr, *Israel: Politics, Myths and Identity Crises* (London and Boulder, Colorado: Pluto Press, 1994).

11. Ze'ev Jabotinsky, founder of Revisionist Zionism, explicitly embraced the idea of a Jewish race (Yaacov Shavit, *Jabotinsky*

and the Revisionist Movement – 1925–1948, London and New Jersey: Frank Cass, 1988, pp. 111–14). In *The Jewish State*, Herzl refers to the Jews as a race, as well as a people and a nation.

12. The First Zionist Congress is described in Chapter 13 of David Vital, *The Origins of Zionism* (Oxford: Oxford University Press, 1975).

13. Alexander Schölch, *Palestine in Transformation 1856–1882* (Washington: Institute for Palestine Studies, 1993). The development of Palestine's trade is discussed on pp. 80–109.

14. Ibid., pp. 284–5. See also Chapter 2, 'Demographic Development', pp. 19–43.

15. Kitty Warnock, *Land Before Honour: Palestinian Women in the Occupied Territories* (Basingstoke and London: Macmillan, 1990) considers the *hamula* in Chapter 2: 'Women's Position in Traditional Society'; Elia Zureik refers to its persistence and role in *The Palestinians in Israel: A Study in Internal Colonialism* (London, Boston and Henley: RKP, 1979). On pp. 136–8, he considers how its influence has been utilised by the Israeli authorities as a means of control over Palestinians in Israel. Marriages to first cousins are still common: according to the Palestinian Central Bureau of Statistics, 27.2 per cent of marriages in the West Bank and 31.6 per cent of those in the Gaza Strip are between first cousins (PCBS Demographic Survey, 1997).

16. 'Honour killings' are an issue which all political factions feel uncomfortable discussing, precisely because so many of the people whose support they want see them as justified. Some also do not want a feature of their society which foreigners would see as very backward to be publicised. The issue has been highlighted in the 1990s by the Israel-based Palestinian feminist organisation, 'Al Fanar'. See interview with Manar Hassan, one of its founders, in *News From Within* (Vol. XI, No. 4, April 1995. *NFW* is published monthly by the Alternative Information Centre, Jerusalem). I have been told on several occasions of women activists being called 'prostitutes', in an attempt by conservative elements in Palestinian society to intimidate them into passivity and conformity. The accusation exposed them to the danger of physical violence by self-appointed guardians of public morality.

17. 'The rate of 30 per cent is regarded as quite reasonable, and is indeed exceeded in many cases' (Sir John Hope Simpson, *Palestine: Report on Immigration, Land Settlement and Development*, London: HMSO, 1930, p. 68).

18.   Khalidi, *Palestinian Identity*, pp. 46–53.
19.   'Aliya' is Hebrew for 'ascent'. It is the term used for the various periods of Jewish immigration to Palestine in modern times. It is indicative of the mystique with which Zionism sought to invest the colonisation of Palestine that it was described in a way which implied that the immigrant was going to some nobler way of life, rather than undertaking a more conventional form of migration. The term 'yerida', meaning 'descent', is used for emigration from Israel, thus investing what would be a normal choice in life elsewhere with shame.
20.   Charles Kamen, *Little Common Ground: Arab Agriculture and Jewish Settlement in Palestine 1920–1948* (Pittsburgh, PA: University of Pittsburgh Press, 1991, p. 185).
21.   Community interaction probably went furthest at Nes Ziyyonah, built next to Arab Wadi Hunin. It was 'unique among all the moshavot: Jews and Arabs lived there together side by side, until the founding of the State of Israel' (Chaim Givati, *A Hundred Years of Settlement*, Jerusalem: Keter Publishing House, 1985, p. 15).
22.   Arthur Ruppin, *The Agricultural Colonisation of the Zionist Organisation in Palestine* (London: Martin Hopkinson, English edition, 1926, pp. 2–3).
23.   Ibid., pp. 5–6.
24.   *History of the Hagana*, p. 860 (Cited in Baruch Kimmerling, *Zionism and Territory*, Berkeley: Institute of International Studies, University of California, 1983, p. 87).
25.   Benjamin Beit-Hallahmi, *Original Sins* (London and Concord, MA: Pluto Press, 1992, p. 186).
26.   In the correspondence between Sir Henry McMahon, British High Commissioner in Cairo and Sharif Hussein of Mecca. The Arab interpretation was later contested by Zionist and some British writers.
27.   The most exhaustive study of the preparation of the Balfour Declaration is Leonard Stein's *The Balfour Declaration* (London: Valentine, Mitchell & Co., 1961).
28.   19 February 1919, FO 371/4179. Cited in A.W. Kayyali, *Palestine: A Modern History* (London: Third World Centre, n.d., p. 64).
29.   Walter Lehn with Uri Davis, *The Jewish National Fund* (London and New York: Kegan Paul International, 1988, pp. 61–4).
30.   See Khalidi, *Palestinian Identity*. He argues convincingly against the view that Palestinian identity emerged solely in reaction to Zionism.

31. The birth of the Palestinian parties and the factional strug-
     gles among Palestinian leaders are treated at length in
     Yehoshua Porat's two volumes, *The Emergence of the
     Palestinian-Arab National Movement 1918–1929* (London and
     New Jersey: Frank Cass, 1974) and *The Palestinian Arab
     National Movement 1929–1939 – From Riots to Rebellion*
     (London and New Jersey: Frank Cass, 1977). Kayyali
     (*Palestine*) also examines these topics.
32. Simon Taggart, *Workers in Struggle: Palestinian Trade Unions
     in the Occupied West Bank* (London: Editpride, 1985, p. 18),
     gives a very brief account of the Palestinian Arab Workers
     Society; Communist criticisms and their own organising
     efforts are described in Musa Budeiri, *The Palestine Communist
     Party 1919–1948* (London: Ithaca Press, 1979), especially
     pp. 185–200.
33. Nira Yuval Davis, *Israeli Women and Men: Divisions Behind the
     Unity* (London: Change Report No. 6. n.d., but evidently
     1981 or just after, pp. 13–14).
34. In a study of the 1967 exodus based on interviews with
     refugees in Zeezya camp, Jordan, 30 out of a sample of 100
     families gave fear of dishonour as a major reason for their
     flight from Palestine (Peter Dodd and Halim Barakat, *River
     Without Bridges*, Beirut: Institute for Palestine Studies, 1968,
     p. 30).
35. Michael Shalev, *Labour and the Political Economy in Israel*
     (Oxford: Oxford University Press, 1992, pp. 39–44).
36. This is a matter of dispute. Kamen, *Little Common Ground*,
     does not accept this interpretation. He points to the evidence
     of interaction between the Arab and Jewish economies and
     argues that pre-partition Palestine should be regarded as one
     economic unit. There is not the space to argue the point
     here, but I think that the degree of separation between the
     Arab and Jewish sectors justifies the use of the term 'dual
     economy'.
37. Shalev, *Labour*, p. 42.
38. Ibid., pp. 99–102.
39. Ze'ev Shiff, *A History of the Israeli Army* (London: Sidgwick
     and Jackson, 1987, p. 6).
40. Ibid., p. 12.
41. Ibid., p. 19; Ilan Pappé, *The Making of the Arab–Israeli Conflict
     1947–1951* (London and New York: I.B. Tauris, 1992, p. 111).
42. This is not to deny that brutalities are committed against
     'enemy' populations as a whole in national conflicts: my

point is that this is exacerbated when other concepts of collective identity – and responsibility – are incorporated into or overlap with that of national identity.

43.   Porat, *Palestinian Arab National Movement 1929–1939,* pp. 132–9.
44.   See Ghassan Kanafani's *Palestine – The 1936–1939 Revolt* (London: Tricontinental Society, n.d. but *c.* 1980, pp. 14–17). Hamas's armed wing is known as the Izz al-Din al-Qassam Battalions.
45.   On the events of the 1936–39 revolt, see Kayyali, *Modern History*, Kanafani, *Palestine* and Porat, *Palestinian Arab National Movement 1929–1939.*
46.   These 'peace bands' were encouraged by the British and the Zionists, of course.
47.   *From Haven to Conquest* (p. xli of Khalidi's introduction and pp. 846–9 of his appendix). The Palestinian Arab losses in the 1936–39 revolt amounted to one in every two hundred of the Arab population.
48.   See Avi Shlaim, *Collusion Across the Jordan – King Abdullah, the Zionist Movement and the Partition of Palestine* (Oxford: Clarendon Press, 1988, pp. 53–65) on the convergence of interests between the Jewish Agency and Abdullah and contacts between them during the revolt.
49.   The Sternists at first used the Irgun's name and later adopted that of 'The Fighters for the Freedom of Israel', known by its Hebrew acronym of LEHI. Their ideology is considered in depth in Joseph Heller, *The Stern Gang: Ideology, Politics and Terror 1940–49* (London and Oregon: Frank Cass, 1995).
50.   Al-Qawukji's recollections of 1948 were published in the summer and autumn 1972 issues (Vol. I, No. 4; Vol. II, No. 1) of the *JPS*. A significantly different impression of the ALA's performance emerges from Nafez Nazzal, *The Palestinian Exodus from Galilee 1948* (Beirut: Institute for Palestine Studies, 1978), based on refugee accounts. Al-Qawukji's most ambitious operation was his attack on Mishmar HaEmek on 4 April 1948. A former resident, Elon Salmon, commented that it 'was saved not so much by the courage of its defenders as by the unbelievable incompetence of Kaukji and his much vaunted Arab Liberation Army' ('Thinking about refugees and the night the Arabs attacked our friendly kibbutz', *The Times*, 19 January 1981).
51.   They were responsible for a succession of terrorist attacks on Palestinian Arabs, and, in particular, carried out the massacre

at Deir Yassin, the most notorious of the acts of brutality which played a decisive role in precipitating the Palestinian exodus in 1948.

52. Netanel Lorch, *The Edge of the Sword: Israel's War of Independence 1947–1949* (New York: G.P. Putnam's Sons, cited in Khalidi, *From Haven to Conquest*, p. 756).
53. Walid Khalidi, *Plan Dalet: The Zionist Master Plan for the Conquest of Palestine* was reproduced in *Why Did the Palestinians Leave?*, published by the Arab League office in London (undated, but probably from the mid-1960s).
54. The 'official' Israeli line has been challenged since the late 1980s by a number of Israeli writers, notably Benny Morris, Avi Shlaim and Ilan Pappé. See especially Morris, *The Birth of the Palestinian Refugee Problem, 1947–1949* (Cambridge: Cambridge University Press, 1988), Avi Shlaim, *Collusion* and Pappé, *Making of the Arab–Israeli Conflict*.

2. A New Nation-State

1. Meir Kahane, the extreme racist leader, responded to Jews who attacked his hostility towards democracy by posing the question of what their attitude would be if 'the Arabs' threatened to become a majority in Israel. Which would be more important to his critics: that the state remained Jewish or that it remained democratic? This proved an effective tactic.
2. Malaria-carrying mosquitoes bred in the marshes around Lake Huleh. It was hoped to solve that problem and create an area of new farmland by draining the lake. The implementation of this scheme projected to the world the kind of images which were dear to the hearts of labour movement Zionists: Jews working the soil and applying modern scientific methods to the task of reclaiming wasteland. This symbolised the 'redemption of the land'. In the long term, it proved ecologically unsound. Fish and birdlife suffered. The reclaimed land had powdery, acidic, infertile soil. The application of large amounts of fertiliser produced contamination downstream in the Jordan and the Sea of Galilee. The area is now being selectively re-flooded.
3. The film of *Exodus* reached an even wider public and made a big impact on Americans in particular. The Haganah hero of the film, Barak Ben Canaan, was played by fair-haired, blue-eyed Paul Newman. This dovetailed with the way in which

Israel chose to project itself to the rest of the world in the 1950s and 1960s. The Israeli army, for example, tended to favour fair-skinned soldiers over those with dark skin in photographic images of itself.

4. Shlomo Swirski, *Israel: The Oriental Majority* (London: Zed Books, 1989) gives a good general account of the position of Oriental Jews in Israel.

5. Just under 250,000 Jews from the Arab world migrated to Israel between 1948 and 1951.

6. Israeli writer, Tom Segev, examined at length the response of government figures, the media and the Israeli public to the arrival of Jews from North Africa and Iraq immediately after the creation of the state. Comments centred on their allegedly primitive, wild and ignorant natures, as well as a supposed predisposition to criminality (Chapter 6, *1949 – The First Israelis*, New York: The Free Press, 1986, pp. 155–94).

7. D. Giladi, *The Palestinian-Jewish Community in the Period of the Fourth Wave of Immigration* (Tel Aviv: Am Oved, 1970, in Hebrew, pp. 51–2, cited in Swirski, *Israel*, p. 10).

8. Ben Gurion was not in the least bit religious and did not take part in a service in a synagogue for the first 40 years that he lived in Palestine (p. 260, Segev, *1949*). The compromises he made with the religious in the first years of Israel's existence would, he hoped, provide an enduring *modus vivendi* for the religious and the non-religious.

9. Don Peretz and Gideon Doron, *The Government and Politics of Israel* (Oxford and Boulder, CO: Westview Press (3rd edition), 1997, pp. 25–6).

10. The Shalit case, which dragged on from 1967 to 1970, had a big impact at the time. Benjamin Shalit, an Israeli Jew serving in the navy, went to the Supreme Court to secure an order that the government should allow his children to be registered as Jewish. They were born to his non-Jewish wife and government officials had refused to record their nationality as 'Jewish' (Israelis are officially identified by nationality and religion, as well as citizenship), as, according to religious law, they were not Jews. The Supreme Court delivered a majority verdict in favour of the Shalits. Prime Minister Golda Meir agreed with leaders of the religious parties that her government would amend the Population Registration Law to declare that, in conformity with Jewish religious law, a person could only be registered as 'Jewish' by nationality if born to a Jewish mother, not adhering to another religious

faith or if converted to Judaism. Chapters 4 and 5 of Akiva Orr, *The UnJewish State* (London: Ithaca Press, 1983) examine this case and its aftermath in detail.

11. David Kretzmer, *The Legal Status of the Arabs in Israel* (Oxford and Boulder, CO: Westview, 1990, pp. 100–2, 106–7).

12. See, inter alia, Sabri Jiryis, *The Arabs in Israel* (New York and London: Monthly Review Press, 1976), Zureik, *Palestinians in Israel* and the series of studies published by Westview in co-operation with the International Centre for Peace in the Middle East, entitled 'The Status and Condition of the Arabs in Israel', of which Kretzmer's study (note 11) forms part.

13. This was reflected in the 1976 Koenig Memorandum, submitted to the Israeli government by the Northern District Commissioner of the Interior Ministry. Koenig argued for measures to cut benefits to large Arab families and for it to be made easier for Arabs to study abroad but harder for them to return.

14. Yoram Peri, *Between Battles and Ballots* (Cambridge: Cambridge University Press, 1983, p. 52, plus footnote 35, p. 298).

15. S.N. Eisenstadt, *The Transformation of Israeli Society* (London: Weidenfeld and Nicolson, 1985, p. 182).

16. '(I)n spite of the substantial drop in the number of regular servicemen and civilian employees in the Israeli army during the last six years, the wage component has increased by about 5 per cent. The improved retirement conditions of the regular servicemen (whose average retirement age is 42 and who receive pensions that are twice as high as that of other state employees whose average retirement age is 61) have increased the military pension budget by 120 per cent in the last decade. Above all, more than 50 per cent of the defence budget is devoted to wages and the service conditions of regular soldiers. This constitutes a rise of over 12 per cent compared with the end of the 1980s. It should be clear that an army that devotes more than half of its budget to wages cannot be an efficient army. The Israeli army is the only army among the democratic states (and maybe even among all countries in the world) that allocates such a big share of its budget just to wages. In the US, for instance, this share is less than 30 per cent.' Reuven Pedatztur, 'The Army Budget and the Next War', *Ha'aretz*, 14 May 1997. I have utilised translations from the Hebrew press made by Israel Shahak, unless otherwise indicated.

17. Two of these death squads are known to have operated during the Intifada. They were known as 'Duvdevan' (Cherry) and 'Shimshon' (Samson) – active in the West Bank and Gaza Strip respectively. They consisted of Israeli soldiers who disguised themselves as Palestinians in order to approach and kill those they were targeting. Squad members were volunteers, including a high proportion of kibbutzniks and regarded as being of the best quality. Between their establishment in 1988 and May 1994, the West Bank human rights organisation, 'Al-Haq', believes that they killed 167 Palestinians (Al-Haq press release, 2 June 1994). Having gunned a person down, they followed what they called 'the procedure of ascertaining a killing', which consisted not of feeling for the victim's pulse, but shooting him in the head at close quarters: there was evidently never any intention of taking that person prisoner. This fact was confirmed when First Sergeant Eli Yisha was accidentally killed by his own colleagues in Jenin on 7 July 1992: grieving relatives spoke to the Israeli press about the manner in which he died (Sima Kadmon, 'The Duvdevan Affair', *Ma'ariv*, 26 February 1993).

18. Benny Morris, 'The Israeli Press and the Qibya Operation, 1953' (*JPS*, No. 100, Summer 1996, pp. 40–52); a number of articles appeared in Israel's Hebrew press in August 1995 on the killings carried out by Israeli troops in 1956: one extended account is Ronal Fisher, 'Mass Murder in the Sinai Sands' (*Ma'ariv*, 8 August 1995); the 1967 murders were described by Arye Yitzhaki, a member of the far-right Tsomet Party (Yossi Melman, 'In the Six Day War the Israeli Army killed some thousand Egyptian soldiers who ceased to function as a combat force', *Ha'aretz*, 17 August 1995). Yitzhaki spoke up because he was annoyed at 'leftists' who were trying to blame his party leader, Rafael Eitan, for the Mitla Pass murders; to make the point that 'leftists' murdered Arabs too, he revealed killings carried out by a unit whose deputy commander was Benjamin Ben Eliezer, Housing Minister in 1995 in the Labour-led government. It is not unusual for ugly details of Israel's past to emerge during sharp exchanges between members of the main Israeli political parties.

19. Israel was the only state to help South Africa's efforts to develop nuclear weapons. The claim that the two states conducted a joint nuclear test in September 1979 was confirmed by Aziz Pahad, post-apartheid South African deputy Foreign

Minister, in an interview with Yossi Melman of *Ha'aretz* (reported in *MidEast Mirror*, 22 April 1997).

20. P.R. Kumaraswamy, 'Recession in Israel's military industries' (*Middle East International,* 7 July 1995).

21. The *Sunday Times* story appeared on 5 October 1986. Much of what Vanunu revealed confirmed what was already known or suspected about Israel's nuclear weapons programme. Nevertheless, he was kidnapped by Israeli agents, tried secretly on treason and 'aggravated espionage' charges, sentenced to 18 years in gaol in March 1988 and imprisoned in conditions of strict isolation – clearly a cruel, punitive rather than security measure, as he had already revealed the information he had.

22. Numerous sympathetic accounts exist of how Israel's armed forces performed in the wars which they fought, such as Chaim Herzog's *The Arab–Israeli Wars* (London and Melbourne: Arms and Armour Press, 1982) and Shiff, *History*. Writers sympathetic to the Palestinians have given comparatively little attention to the topic. A couple of exceptions are Clifford Wright, 'The Israeli War Machine in Lebanon' (*JPS*, No. 46, Winter 1983) and Yezid Sayigh, 'Israel's Military Performance in Lebanon, June 1982' (*JPS*, No. 49, Fall 1983).

23. Literature on the Israeli intelligence services used to range from the adulatory to the merely uncritical. Among the better, more recent books on them are Dan Raviv and Yossi Melman, *Every Spy A Prince* (Boston, London and Melbourne: Dan Houghton Mifflin Company, 1990) and Ian Black and Benny Morris, *Israel's Secret Wars – A History of Israel's Intelligence Services* (London: Futura, 1992).

24. CIA, *Israel: Foreign Intelligence and Security Services*, March 1979, p. 10.

25. Ibid., p. 21: 'The Israeli intelligence service depends heavily on the various Jewish communities and organisations abroad for recruiting agents and eliciting general information. The aggressively ideological nature of Zionism, which emphasizes that all Jews belong to Israel and must return to Israel, had had its drawbacks in enlisting support for intelligence operations, however, since there is considerable opposition to Zionism among Jews throughout the world. Aware of this fact, Israeli intelligence representatives usually operate discreetly within Jewish communities and are under instructions to handle their missions with utmost tact to avoid embarrassment in Israel. They also attempt to penetrate anti-

Zionist elements in order to neutralize the opposition. Despite such precautions, the Israelis frequently experience setbacks and there have been several cases where attempted recruitments of Americans of the Jewish faith have been rejected and reported to the US authorities.'

26. 'Spooking the Spooks', Julian Borger and Ian Black, *Guardian*, 13 October 1997.

27. In February 1987, the Alternative Information Centre (AIC) was closed for six months by an order issued under the Prevention of Terrorism Ordinance. It was accused of serving as a front for the Popular Front for the Liberation of Palestine. Its director, Michel Warshawski, was subsequently found guilty of only one of the four charges made against him: that of providing typesetting services for the production of a booklet on the interrogation methods of the Shabak. In January 1989, the four Jewish editors of *Derech Hanitzotz* were convicted of membership of a terrorist organisation (the Democratic Front for the Liberation of Palestine) and membership of and providing a service to an illegal organisation, following plea bargaining.

28. Nahum Barnea, 'Nafsu: Prisoner without a name, trial without a witness' (*Koteret Rashit*, 23 April 1987, published in English in the AIC's bulletin, *News From Within*, 20 May 1987).

29. The story of Shabak's behaviour in the 'Bus 300' affair was covered at some length as it unfolded by *News From Within* in 1986 and 1987. The two works mentioned in note 23, above, deal with the Nafsu and 'Bus 300' affairs.

30. Much has been written on the Landau Commission. *The Interrogation of Palestinians During the Intifada: Ill-treatment, 'Moderate Physical Pressure' or Torture?* (B'Tselem – The Israeli Information Center for Human Rights in the Occupied Territories, 1991) describes the main findings of the report and considers its practical implications in depth. Stanley Cohen, 'Torture in Israel: Defining the Issues' (*New Outlook*, September 1990) is a brief but hard-hitting critique of the Landau Commission's report.

31. Jiryis, *Arabs*, pp. 83–8.

32. Ibid., p. 95. Two chapters of Jiryis's book are devoted to describing the seizure of Palestinian Arab land in Israel and the legal measures used to justify it.

33. Adam Keller, *Terrible Days – Social Divisions and Political Paradoxes in Israel* (Amsterdam: Cypres, 1987, pp. 191–6).

34. Oded Liphshitz, 'Arabs, Don't Appeal to the Supreme Court' (*Hotam*, 31 July 1987).

3. Renewal and Retreat

1. Rosemary Sayigh, *Palestinians: From Peasants to Revolutionaries* (London: Zed Books, 1979) focuses on the Palestinians in Lebanon, giving accounts of their attitudes and experiences. In *Too Many Enemies: The Palestinian Experience in Lebanon* (London and New Jersey: Zed Books, 1994) she builds on her earlier work, this time concentrating on the lives of the inhabitants of Shatila refugee camp in Beirut.
2. Aida Karaoglan, *The Struggle Goes On* (Beirut: PLO Research Centre, 1969, p. 144). Arafat is here known by his *nom de guerre*, Abu Ammar.
3. Ann Mosely Lesch, 'The Gaza Strip: Heading Toward a Dead End' (Hanover, NH: *UFSI Reports*, No. 10, 1984, p. 3).
4. The most useful single account of the PLO's development is Helena Cobban, *The Palestinian Liberation Organisation – People, Power and Politics* (Cambridge: Cambridge University Press, 1984). *Free Palestine* (published monthly in London, 1968–1981), *JPS*, *Palestine* (published by the PLO intermittently and at varying frequencies) and the magazines of the PFLP and DFLP (*Democratic Palestine* and *DFLP Bulletin*, respectively, neither published any more), as well as innumerable conversations and articles all provided source material on the political perspectives of the major Palestinian organisations.
5. 'Strategy in China's Revolutionary War' (*Selected Works of Mao Tse Tung, Volume I*, Peking: Foreign Languages Press, 1967, p. 211).
6. Sayigh, *Palestinians*, pp. 163–75
7. This was envisaged under the Allon Plan, the first version of which was prepared by Yigal Allon and submitted to the Israeli cabinet in July 1967. It was never officially accepted as government policy under Labour, but it did serve as a guide to where the government established settlements in the West Bank. Under the plan, Israel would annex the land it held in the Jordan valley, except for a corridor around Jericho linking the West Bank with Jordan. It would also annex an area around Jerusalem and the Latrun salient. The densely populated Arab areas would form part of a state based on the

East Bank. In 1997, officials close to Netanyahu described his plans for the future of the West Bank as 'Allon Plan minus', indicating that the Palestinians were to be allowed a smaller area of land than Allon had envisaged would go to a Palestinian-Jordanian state.

8. The text of the 1964 version of the Palestine National Charter is reproduced in *The Arab–Israeli Conflict* (Vol. III, ed. John Norton Moore, Princeton: Princeton University Press, 1974, pp. 699–704).

9. For the text of the Palestine National Charter as revised in 1968, see *Basic Political Documents* (ed. Leila S. Kadi, p. 137).

10. 'Political Statement Issued by the Sixth Palestine National Assembly', in *International Documents on Palestine, 1969* (Ed. Walid Khadduri, Beirut: Institute for Palestine Studies and Kuwait: University of Kuwait, 1972, p. 779).

11. For example, in Dr Mohammad Rasheed, *Towards a Democratic State in Palestine* (Beirut: PLO Research Centre, 1970, pp. 9 and 35).

12. *JPS*, No. 12, Summer 1974, p. 224.

13. *JPS*, No. 70, Winter 1989, p. 214.

14. The PLO's strongest links with other liberation movements were with organisations like the ANC, which enjoyed very broad international support and with movements against dictatorial regimes backed by the USA, such as the Sandinistas in Nicaragua.

15. This emerged in a discussion with an EPLF representative in 1990: I have not seen it in print.

16. See Chapters 6 and 7, Gérard Chaliand, *The Palestinian Resistance* (Harmondsworth: Penguin, 1972, pp. 84–129).

17. I have been involved in the Palestine solidarity movement since 1969: my observations are based on that experience.

18. 'NGO Appeal for an International Peace Conference on the Middle East' (Special Non-Governmental Organizations' Bulletin, New York: United Nations Division for Palestinian Rights, 85-01603, January 1985). The appeal was adopted at the First International NGO Meeting on the Question of Palestine on 20–22 August 1984; a variation was to call for the participation of the five permanent members of the Security Council, rather than just the USA and USSR.

19. Abu Iyad with Eric Rouleau, *My Home, My Land: A Narrative of the Palestinian Struggle* (New York: Times Books, 1981, p. 43).

20. Outlined in *Political and Armed Struggle* (Fatah, no publication details, but probably in Amman late in 1969).

21. This was not admitted by Abu Iyad, but he did say that he knew a number of Black September members, who 'belonged to various fedayeen organisations. Coming out of the ranks, they accurately reflected the profound feelings of frustration and indignation shared by the entire Palestinian people regarding the Jordanian massacres and the complicities that made them possible.' He hinted at the tactical character of the organisation's activities: 'Black September ... acted as an auxiliary of the Resistance, when the Resistance was no longer in a position to fully assume its military and political tasks.' Abu Iyad, Eric Rouleau, *My Home*, p. 98.
22. Ibid., p. 214.
23. Chapter 5 of Noam Chomsky, *The Fateful Triangle: The United States, Israel and the Palestinians* (London: Pluto Press, 1983) provides an excellent polemical analysis of Israel's professed reasons for its invasion of Lebanon and its real reasons.
24. Israel tries to take credit for the fact that five universities – now six – exist where there were none before 1967, but in fact they were all created by the efforts of Palestinians or sympathetic outsiders – the Vatican, in the case of Bethlehem.
25. When the Intifada ended is a point of political controversy. Fatah withdrew from the UNLU after the DoP was signed and regarded the Intifada as then at an end. The PFLP and DFLP talked about continuing the Intifada for months afterwards, when it was obviously over. I recall listening to Palestinian activists from the West Bank in autumn 1991 casually talking about the Intifada in the past tense.
26. Rema Hammami, 'Women, the Hijab and the Intifada' (Washington: *Middle East Report*, Nos 164–5, May–August 1990, pp. 24–8) gives a sound analysis of the struggle over the wearing of headscarves by women.

4. A New Stage?

1. It might be objected that this judgement is premature, as, at the time of writing, the negotiations between Israel and the PLO have not been concluded. I believe the statement to be justified.

   The modern Palestinian national movement's early aims – the 'liberation of Palestine' or a 'democratic, non-sectarian state of Palestine' were dropped by the PLO in favour of the 'two state solution'. According to the decisions of the 19th

PNC meeting in 1988, this was meant to involve a full Israeli withdrawal from all the Palestinian territory occupied by Israel in 1967, including East Jerusalem. The withdrawal meant not only the removal of soldiers, but also of Israeli settlers. The Palestinians were to enjoy full statehood. The refugees were to be allowed to return home and/or receive compensation.

There is no prospect of this being achieved through the DoP. In theory, the PLO and Israel accept UN Security Council Resolutions 242 and 338 as the basis for a permanent settlement, but all Israeli governments to date have rejected the idea that Israel is obliged to withdraw from all the territories it occupied in 1967 under the terms of 242. None have been prepared to countenance Israeli withdrawal from East Jerusalem; neither the Netanyahu government nor its Labour predecessors have been prepared to discuss the issue of Palestinian refugees in the terms of UN General Assembly Resolution 194 of 1948, which stated that refugees willing to live in peace with their neighbours should be allowed to return to their homes and that compensation should be paid to those choosing not to return. During the 'peace process', the expansion of Israeli settlements in the West Bank and the construction of roads to serve them which by-pass Palestinian population centres has continued. It is clear that Israel intends to keep the majority of settlements under its control, as well as the roads giving access to them, which fragment the territory upon which Palestinians hope to establish an independent state.

The DoP provided a framework within which negotiations for final Israeli–Palestinian peace settlement could take place, but it did not mandate that they should be based upon international law or upon UN resolutions pertaining to Palestine/Israel (apart from 242 and 338). The outcome of the talks will depend upon the balance of power between the PLO and Israel and, in the absence of determined pressure upon Israel from the West, particularly the USA, the PLO is in a very weak position. At the time of writing, it appears that the best deal it can obtain, even from a new Labour-led government, is a Palestinian entity with the title of 'state', but without all of the powers of an independent state and authority over a mere 10 per cent or so of historic Palestine. Most of the Palestinians in exile in Lebanon, Syria, Jordan and elsewhere will be condemned to remain outside their homeland. This can not be called anything other than a defeat.

Index

Index compiled by Auriol Griffith-Jones